Bending Bamboo
Changing Winds

Nepali Women Tell Their Life Stories

Written and compiled by

Eva Kipp

With contributions from

Kim Hudson
Lucia de Vries
Marieke van Vliet
Alieke Barmentloo

PILGRIMS PUBLISHING
VARANASI   DELHI   KATHMANDU

Bending Bamboo Changing Winds: Nepali Women Tell Their Life Stories
Eva Kipp

Published by
PILGRIMS PUBLISHING
An imprint of
PILGRIMS BOOK HOUSE
(Distributors in India)
B 27/98 A-8, Nawabganj Road
Durga Kund, Varanasi 221005, India
Phones: 91-542-2314060, 2314060   Fax: 2312788
e-mail: pilgrims@satyam.net.in
Website: www.pilgrimsbooks.com

PILGRIMS BOOK HOUSE
1626 Raj Guru Road, ChunaMandi
Pahar Ganj, New Delhi 110055, India
Phones: 91-11-23584019, 23584015   Fax: 23584015
e-mail: pilgrimsinde@gmail.com

Edited by
Daniel Bayard Haber

All photographs except chapters 4, 6, and 13 by
Eva Kipp

Cover artwork of first edition by
Eva Kipp

Endpaper drawings by
Hira Karna

First Published B F I 1995
Second Edition
Copyright (c) 2006, Pilgrims Publishing
All Rights Reserved

Editing, layout and resetting of this edition by
Astricks, New Delhi, www.astricks.com

ISBN: 81-7769-451-0

Process & Printed at : Surya Print Process Pvt. Ltd., New Delhi (India)

*Dedicated
to all the women
of Nepal*

*Like bamboo, graceful, upright and strong,
women bend and grow,
adjusting to the winds of change.*

Inspired by the ancient Chinese philosophy *Tao Te Ching* by Lao Tzu

Contents

Preface

The idea for this book came up during a workshop on Gender and Development that took place in April 1994, which was organised by SNV Nepal (Netherlands Development Organisation).

For this workshop six gender studies were carried out in areas where SNV Nepal is working. Collecting life histories of Nepalese village women was a part of the research. It was found that the life histories gave an enormous insight into how Nepali women in different cultural and environmental circumstances live and think. Our goal was to talk with women living in different parts of Nepal and to study to what extent changes have taken place in their traditional lives.

The plan to have such a book compiled and edited was mooted by Mrs Riet Turksma, Women and Development Specialist of the Royal Netherlands Embassy in Delhi. The 'Women and Development Fund Local' of the Royal Netherlands Embassy in Delhi provided financial support to make the publication of the book possible.

Preface to the second edition

I feel satisfied that the second edition of *Bending Bamboo* has come about. Since the publication of the first edition more than ten years ago, there has been a sustained demand for the book worldwide. I have not changed any essential parts of the text, but the book has been re-edited, has a different layout, and a new cover.

Acknowledgments

The other authors and I would like to express our sincere appreciation and gratitude for the time and generous hospitality offered by all the women we interviewed, and for the frank and honest way in which they were prepared to share with us extremely personal details of their lives.

I would also like to thank the following organisations that facilitated the interviewing in various ways: the SNV Nepal (Netherlands Development Organisation), the Annapurna Conservation Area Project (ACAP), the Women's Development Organisation (WOREC), Institute for Integrated Development Studies (IIDS) and Lutheran World Service (LWS). We especially appreciate the assistance from the Language Training Institute (LTI), notably from Mr Hem B. Rai, Mr Dilip K. Sainju, Mr Rajendra Sapkota and Mrs Parmeswari Shrestha, who helped with the research and translations of the interviews.

Furthermore, I wish to thank Mrs Riet Turksma of the Royal Netherlands Embassy in Delhi for all her support and encouragement; without the financial grant from the Royal Netherlands Embassy our original ideas would never have been turned into a reality. As the co-author and coordinator of the project I got contributions of various kinds from three researchers and a journalist who were also present at the workshop on Gender and Development held in April 1994. All contributed with some life histories. Kim Hudson, Lucia de Vries and Daniel Haber have contributed considerably in the process of editing. The work of SNV Nepal facilitated contacts with the village women who, along with other NGOs, helped make this book possible.

I am grateful to my husband Mr Eric Kamphuis for his factual and moral support.

Finally, I express my sincere thanks to Mr Rama Nand and Mr John Snyder Jr. of Pilgrims Publishing for a fruitful collaboration.

Eva Kipp

Map of Nepal:
Homes of the Women Interviewed

Introduction

This book has been written with the purpose of gaining a greater understanding of the reality of Nepali women's life in different parts of the country, in varied socio-economic categories, and also, in most cases, how positive changes in their lives have taken place.

Visiting the women and talking with them yielded a wealth of information and a glimpse into their lives, thoughts, beliefs, concerns and pleasures — factors which rarely appear in statistics. The women showed remarkable resourcefulness in developing strategies to cope with conditions and situations that seem very difficult to outsiders. Nepal is a small, mountainous kingdom populated by a variety of ethnic groups of Aryan and Mongolian stock. The varied topography of high mountains, low plains and inaccessible valleys has restricted communications between the many indigenous groups and outsiders, so that ancient languages and dialects, as well as religious beliefs and customs, have been preserved and the differences across the country are vast.

For a Nepali woman the group into which she is born often determines the whole pattern of her life. Her position, status and freedom depends on the laws and characteristics of her ethnic group. Women belonging to the Mongolian (Tibeto-Burman) groups like Sherpa, Gurung and Tamang generally have fewer restrictions than the women belonging to the Indo-Aryan groups such as Brahmin, Chhetri and Newar, where child marriage still exists and the position of a daughter-in-law is still very unfavourable.

The religion of the Indo-Aryan groups is Hindu, and these groups are divided into castes. In medieval times the country used only indigenous labour to meet all its needs. In order to attain self-sufficiency, divisions were made in the society and tasks allocated to particular groups, known as castes. Castes are hereditary and the caste system is hierarchical. Skills were handed down through generations. Skilled craftsmen and artisans, such as blacksmiths, shoemakers and tailors, were given the lowest ranking in the hierarchy and regarded as 'untouchable'.

Despite the formal abolition of the caste system in 1963 and the diversification of trade and callings of people within the different castes, it has proved very difficult to shake off the age-old customs and legacy of the past. Members of the higher castes tend to be more resistant to change than lower caste people who continue to face discrimination. The former system of marriage, restricted to one's own caste, is now breaking down in some parts of the country, as an increasing number of young people choose their own partners. More progressive families may accept a daughter-in-law whom they have not selected themselves, even if she is from a different caste, but more traditional families may refuse, leaving the newly married couple to fend for themselves.

A Hard Life in the Hills

Nepal has a predominantly agricultural economy and it is generally estimated that about ninety per cent of the population depends on agriculture as their main source of livelihood. Nevertheless, here also, many changes are taking place.

The rapidly increasing population puts high demands on the limited land available, particularly in the hills, thus causing environmental degradation, depletion of resources and subsequent decreases in income from subsistence farming livelihood. Production of rain-fed agriculture is no longer sufficient to meet the needs of a family throughout the year and commodities such as sugar, soap and kerosene must be purchased with cash. The male members of the household therefore often emigrate from the hills down to the plains or further south to India to find paid employment.

In a labour-intensive subsistence economy the workload of women is normally higher than that of men, and children also contribute to the tasks necessary for family survival. Due to the migration of working males, most women and children in the hills are left on their own for many months of the year, even several years at a time while their husbands and relatives seek wage labour as guards or porters. In many cases, women are the de jure heads of the household due to the death, desertion or second marriage of their husband's. There are also many women who are the de facto heads of their household due to the temporary absence of their male partners. These women have the sole responsibility of all crop, livestock and household management, as well as the rearing of the children.

The economic condition of households, especially those headed by a woman, varies depending on the composition and location of the household, the ages of the family members, the access to, and control over the resources available to the women and the attitude and degree of cooperation within the community. Household incomes often fall below the poverty line where there is no adult income to support the family, and the likelihood of children being able to attend school decreases. Some children may be sent to work in a factory, usually carpet factories in areas far away from home. Girls may be given away in marriage at an early age, or even sold to reduce the number of mouths to feed. Women who are forced to seek wage labour are generally exploited, as any complaint about pay or conditions will result in the loss of their income and means of support. In some areas young women from poor families, often deceived by false promises of good jobs, go to India to work and end up in the brothels, as prostitutes.

Changes

In modern Nepalese society many changes influencing the lives of women are taking place. In the past, women's lives were directed by social and cultural norms, and although traditional customs still play an important role in their lives, many new things have emerged. Women now have access to education, improved services such as water supply and health care, and opportunities to travel. Projects focusing on methods to increase women's income have improved the quality of life and provided alternate strategies for survival for both women and their families. Tourism has brought villagers into contact with other lifestyles and provided economic improvement and new business opportunities.

Technological changes have influenced their lives too. For example, Hindi film songs from radios, and cassettes are replacing traditional songs, and television is now replacing the old forms of family entertainment in the evenings. The status and position of village women in Nepal is gradually changing in many areas and, portrayed by statistics, women's lives would seem to have improved over the last twenty years. Female literacy has increased more than six-fold, the average age of marriage has increased from fifteen to eighteen years and the life expectancy of a woman in Nepal has risen from forty-two years in 1961 to fifty-two, at the time of writing.

However, a closer examination of the statistics and conversations with rural women also reveal deterioration in women's lives in many cases. The gap between the literacy rates of males and females continues to increase, access to higher education is still limited for girls, few women reach the top in administrative roles and a mere handful have risen to a position of political power. The maternal mortality rate is still one of the highest in the world. To illustrate, we excerpt the tragic story of Ganga Devi Rajbanshi from Dhangadi:

Ganga Devi was pregnant with her fourth child. The night after she had been to see the doctor, an unbearable pain started. As is practiced in some areas in Nepal, Ganga Devi delivered alone:

> 'The baby was lying sideways and not moving at all. The pain was intolerable which led me to cut my abdomen, or else why does anybody do such a thing? This happened only because I could not bear the pain.'

> 'I pulled the baby out and later found the baby was dead.' Ganga Devi Rajbanshi died three weeks later.*

* Interview by Kedar Sharma taken from the Nepali television programme 'Peeping Window' produced by the Environment Journalist Association, broadcast on 24 May 1994.

The law states that a woman cannot inherit the property of her parents unless she is still unmarried at the age of thirty-five. Women, therefore, have little economic security unless their parents are rich and generous and their husband is hard working and faithful. They therefore depend very much on their sons who, traditionally, remain in the joint family after marriage. Thus a woman's capacity to bear sons plays a very important role in Nepalese society from the point of view of both parents and grandparents. Village women often quote an old proverb, which says:

> *A house with two women is a reliable house.*
> *A house with two sons is a reliable house.*
> *A house with two oxen is a reliable house.*

Women's Reaction to Change

When confronted with changes in their personal circumstances or in traditional village life, women display incredible inventiveness and usually make maximum use of new opportunities in order to improve their own lives, especially the lives of their children.

Women in Nepal not only attempt to change their immediate living conditions for their own good but also make long-term improvements to various aspects of life in their society so that everyone will benefit. This was the case of a number of women interviewed for this book. One woman, Rukmani Shrestha, having once suffered herself, is now working hard to improve the unhygienic practices of the traditional birth attendants in her village. Thus, she hopes to reduce the unnecessary suffering of numerous mothers. Another woman, Jagan Gurung, helped local women to organise themselves in groups in order to carry out development activities in their communities. When lots of tourists started coming to her village, Jagan also opened a new lodge with an approach based on sound ecological principles to show others how the deforestation of the local area might be avoided.

Maya Lama is trying to explain the devastating effects of AIDS to young girls in her village after her experiences in a brothel in Bombay.

Long before the intervention of development aid from outside the country women were devising their own ways of coping with personal and economic needs but the advent of projects in the recent years has increased access to means of economic independence for women. Anuragi Jha, originally forbidden to leave the confines of her home, used to make traditional Maithili paintings on her own walls. She is now working as an artist in a local project, travels about on her own and no longer has to ask anyone else for money. Man Maya Balampaki Magar has found sericulture an ideal occupation for her old age after a project started in her local area.

Some women, however, as a result of rigid traditions, gender imbalance and misfortune, lack the opportunities to improve their situation. These women often belong to the disadvantaged groups such as the 'untouchable' castes and the landless, for whom life is still a hard struggle for survival.

A remarkable fact which emerges from the stories, is the lengths which women will go to improve the life of their children. Women have crossed physical barriers, traditional and economic restrictions, in order to give their children a good education. Some, as in the case of Lamseki Sherpa, have decided to give up their traditional way of life in the high pastures, as this meant their children could not go to school. Anuragi Jha ignored the disapproval of in-laws and community and set up a small shop in order to pay for her children to attend school.

In compiling this book, women were chosen from the many ethnic groups and castes found in Nepal and a further selection was made according to their specific lifestyles and activities. Most of the women come from a background of poverty and have had little or no education. Personal visits were paid to all women, and a considerable length of time, varying from a few days to a few weeks, was spent discussing their problems with them in their homes. Usually, confidence grew and the women relaxed as questions were asked while they went about their daily chores such as fetching water or even digging roots in the forest. Some women hardly felt inhibited at all and would tell us their life histories in an almost uninterrupted stream of words or share intimate details even though we had only just met.

Listening to village women helps us to identify and understand the elements which have contributed to positive changes in their lives. We have to take into account diverse factors such as personality, sociological conditioning associated with a particular ethnic group, caste, the availability and use of opportunities for change and the access to and control over resources such as property and money and how these can influence women's ability to take charge of their own lives. Those factors which obstruct women as they strive to improve the lives of their families can also be isolated and taken into consideration before any form of intervention takes place.

From their life histories one can learn what women think about different aspects of their lives and the changes that are taking place. It also shows how powerful and creative village women can be.

A song from the singer Malewa Devi expresses the conflicting views about the worth of women in Nepal:

> *There is no building needed to have a house,*
> *The women herself is the home.*
> *Women, the only source of cosmic law,*
> *She is the gate of the home.*

The women is the goddess of the home,
But she is also the slave of the home.
She is the queen and the diamond of the home,
You enjoy heaven which is worth achieving,
While being the goddess Laxmi and the minister of the home.

Devotion to Duty

Newari women lining up to offer food and flowers

1

Rukmani Shrestha
Devotion to Duty

THIMI IS SITUATED in the Kathmandu valley near Bhaktapur and is one of the larger settlements in the valley with a population of about 17,000. Most inhabitants are Newar although a few hill people, such as Tamangs, have migrated to Thimi and there are some non-Newar low caste groups living in the area. Most houses in Thimi are built in typical Newari style many storeys high and nestling close together along narrow cobbled streets and alleys. The brick-built houses have intricately carved wooden doors and windows and roofs of small clay tiles.

Thimi is famous for the pottery of low caste Newars, known as *Kuma*, who make a wide range of products from simple flowerpots and water jugs to miniature clay menageries including elephants and peacocks. This work is done outside in the open courtyards and the pots are dried in the sun before baking. Together with the old Newar houses, the cobbled streets and the temples, the pottery-making adds to the quaint atmosphere.

The Newars are the original inhabitants of the Kathmandu valley and still make up the majority of the population. Newars distinguish themselves from other groups in Nepal by their own language, caste system and their rich culture. Most of them are traders, businessmen or skilled artisans. They celebrate many colourful festivals and have special rituals for boys and girls for initiation into adulthood.

In Nepal the rates for both infant and maternal mortality are high. Birth is generally considered to be polluting, and according to ancient customs, many women deliver alone outside the house under unhygienic conditions that endanger the life of both child and mother. Among the Newars there are also strong traditional practices surrounding childbirth. One example is the

An example of a typical Newari brick-built house with an intricately carved wooden window

custom of placing the placenta in a clay pot, performing a ceremony of worship and only cutting the umbilical cord on the third or fourth day after delivery.

In many areas of Nepal a *sudeni*, or traditional birth attendant, will assist with deliveries. Usually these women have no formal training, just experience. In Newar society the traditional midwives are also *jhankris* (faith healers) but these women are not always fully aware of the importance of hygiene. They are also afraid they will lose prestige if they have to send women to a hospital, even in the case of severe complications. Nowadays, training for midwives is being organised to improve traditional practices.

Rukmani Shrestha

We first meet Rukmani Shrestha in the front of the family pharmacy by a busy road and retreat into the courtyard at the rear of the building to escape from the noise of passing vehicles. She is

Rukmani Shrestha

quiet and modest yet exudes confidence. She is wearing a sari and a dark shawl which makes her look rather tired and pale but this look disappears as soon as she starts to talk and laugh.

Rukmani does most of the cleaning and cooking in the house. She also works on the land, looks after the family pharmacy and works as a midwife. Her husband is an ayurvedic doctor and *jhankri* and consults patients at home. The family has some land and hires workers to cultivate wheat and rice which is used to make *chiura*. Rice for cooking is bought in the shops.

She takes us to a family where she had helped deliver a baby some days earlier. We are invited in for tea and *chhyang* and sit on the roof with some women and their two small children. Rukmani talks with the young mother and holds the baby, the expression on her face revealing genuine interest in her work. The women comment that Rukmani is always willing to come when they ask, is never too busy and is always patient and friendly. They feel at ease with her and know they can rely on her.

Rukmani Tells Her Story

My First Baby

I gave birth to my first child after two years of marriage when I was twenty-two years old. At that time I had not yet done my training in midwifery so I had no idea what would happen. My mother-in-law who is a *chaimani*, a traditional midwife and spirit healer, helped during the delivery together with some female neighbours. Before the baby was born they lit a fire outside the room and I was given a sweet snack of *ghee* (clarified butter), ginger and brown sugar to make me feel warm inside and help the contractions. To ensure that all went well people chanted a few ancient sayings and I was beaten on my stomach with my sari. Oil was rubbed onto my belly and, later, onto my breasts as the nipples were closed.

I was in labour for twenty-four hours, and remember thinking that perhaps it would be better to die than to have such awful pains. I didn't realise that they were part of the delivery — I thought I was the only one who had ever had them! Later on, I saw other women suffering and now I realise that the pain forces one to get on with the delivery.

My parents were in another room in the same house. My mother was not allowed to see me as it is thought that a mother should not see her daughter in pain. They wanted me to be taken to the hospital but my mother-in-law refused because she thought that it might damage her reputation as a midwife. Luckily, however, there were no serious problems, except for a small tear for which I needed medication, and finally I gave birth to a daughter. I was very pleased with her.

To help deliver the placenta one of the women put my hand in my mouth to make me retch. The placenta came out without any problem ten minutes later; it was put in a clay pot and then 'worshipped' with grains of rice and *chiura*. A woman of the *Kata* caste came to cut the umbilical cord. I'm not sure what she used — I didn't even look to see if it was clean: in those days I was not aware of what I know now. After the delivery I had to drink a bowl of *musto*, a mixture of mustard oil and clarified butter.

When my second daughter was born I didn't mind, but after delivering my third daughter I felt rather disappointed. Finally, when I had a son I became very happy. Our people prefer sons to daughters because all the wealth of the parents goes to the son or sons after the parents die. A son does not leave the house when he marries but will bring home a daughter-in-law, whereas a daughter will leave her parental home after her wedding to join her husband and his family. Furthermore, a son is required to perform all the rituals for his parents after their death. If a son is born the parents believe they will be able to go to heaven because the proper rituals can be done but, if they don't have a son, they're not sure if they will go to heaven.

Handing Over the Baby

For six days after the birth, the mother and baby are considered polluted and, therefore, untouchable. On the sixth day, a purification ritual is performed after the mother and baby have been washed, and the midwife comes to take part in the ritual. We believe that the newborn 'belongs' to the midwife and that, only on the day of purification, does she formally 'hand it over'. The father has to follow the ancient custom of giving her some money and then he can take his child. The midwife must also perform a small puja for the mother and baby too. The mother's mother is also be present on that day and gives food and new clothes to both baby and mother. When all the rituals have been performed the child finally belongs to the parents. For this day we make all sorts of delicious food but before eating we put some food on a large leaf plate, and put it outside the house to appease any local ghosts and demons.

A name is given to the child according to the horoscope but this name is not used in daily life. There is no matter of liking the name or not, it has to be given depending on the date and time of birth. Another name will be given for use in daily life and this does not require any special ceremony. In Newar society the new mother does not have to do any work for two months. The mother and the baby get massaged with oil twice a day and the mother is given rice, meat and butter three times a day along with green vegetables. My eldest sister-in-law gave me massages after my deliveries and, in turn, I massaged her when she delivered her child — in Thimi we don't call in special women to do this.

My Early Life

I was born in Thimi forty-five years ago. I am the eldest child and have three brothers and one sister; we had two more brothers but they died. My parents sent all of us to school but I also had to help with the chores at home and on the land. I studied up to the sixth class and then stopped. I preferred playing to studying and my grandmother told me, since I could read, write and do some basic arithmetic, that was enough. For the next five years I didn't read or write. There was no secondary school in those days, later one was built, and my friends started going, I decided that I should go too. In the beginning I felt shy about going back to school but I got used to it. My parents were happy to send my brothers to school but they wanted me to stay at home to do the housework. They were probably scared that I would elope with a boy as well, however, I made sure I did my chores quickly so I had time to study.

My mother is from a village and did not go to school. My father studied up to the sixth class and can speak a bit of English. He was a driver in Kathmandu for twenty years and then gave it up to take over the running of a teashop from his father. My parents own some land as well.

Into Adulthood

In Newar society we have special ceremonies to celebrate our passing into adulthood. One day when I was twelve years old my mother said to me, 'You are a big girl, now you have to go through the ritual of *gupha basne*, (literally — to stay in a cave). For twelve days I was not allowed to see the sun or any male persons and I had to stay inside the house. My friends visited me and we played with stones and sang love songs from the traditional dramas that were performed in Thimi once a year in those days. They were all tragic love stories. I'll sing you one of those songs:

> *I planted a flower of love in my heart for you.*
> *But why should I bring this flower to you?*
> *It is still a bud and has to become a blossoming flower.*
> *Why not wait until it is . . . ?*

On the twelfth day I was dressed in beautiful clothes and adorned with jewellery. We went to the temple of Ganesh and there a Brahmin priest performed the rituals. He unveiled my face and showed me the sun, then I was given a vermilion mark on my hair. Guests were invited and we ate and sang. Having done the *gupha* rituals I knew that something should happen that had to do with becoming an adult woman but I was not sure what. How could I know? I was fifteen years old when I menstruated for the first time — I felt perplexed and ashamed. I knew that in this condition I was regarded as impure and, therefore, not allowed to enter the kitchen, touch the gods or worship, so I had to inform my mother but I did not dare. Only in the evening did I find the courage to tell her.

We Newari girls actually 'marry' three times, first with the fruit of the *bel* tree, then with the sun god *Surya Bhagawan* and, at last, we marry a man! This custom ensures that we do not have to face the stigma of being a widow. My husband was my private English teacher. We fell in love

8

Newari mother performing puja by the Ganesh temple
on the last day of the young girls' ceremony of *'gupha basne'*

and married when I was twenty years old. At that time he had a room in Kathmandu and I used to visit him regularly on the pretext that I was going to Kathmandu to go to the Pashupatinath temple.

We went through the simple *swayambar* marriage ritual at the Guhyashwori temple exchanging garlands of flowers. My husband put *sindur*, a red powder, on the parting in my hair — a sign that I was now married. We had no witnesses, but my husband said, 'Look at all those monkeys — they are our witnesses!' A week later I went to Dhulikhel to see my husband and from there we went to Kathmandu and lived together in his room. My mother became suspicious, but when my father asked her where I was she replied that I was staying with relatives.

My husband's family used to give him a small sack of rice every week, but one day, my husband's brother came to visit and seeing me in the room, he realised that we were married. From that day on everyone in the family knew about it. My husband's family, and mother-in-law in particular, were very angry and no longer provided the measure of rice, so we didn't have enough food. My father was also unhappy as it damaged his status in society, but once my mother had met my husband, she did not mind.

In our society, in which almost everybody has an arranged marriage, it is difficult to have a 'love marriage' mainly because of the caste system and the economic situation. In the eyes of both families the girl loses her honour even if there is no difference in caste between the boy and girl.

Training to be a Midwife

After my second daughter was born I decided to go to the University Nursing Campus for training in midwifery. I had started to go along with my mother-in-law whenever she attended a delivery but I always worried that there would be complications and I wouldn't be able to cope. That is what prompted me to study. My husband was very supportive and thought it would be good for me — better than sitting at home — and so my mother-in-law gave her permission. I worked for fourteen months in the Kathmandu Maternity Hospital. Altogether the training was two-and-a-half years and afterwards I worked outside the valley for a further three years. When I became pregnant again I asked to be transferred to Kathmandu but they refused, so I left my job.

Life with Mother-in-Law

When we returned to Kathmandu we lived with my mother-in-law, my husband's other two brothers and their families. There were lots of quarrels, as my mother-in-law and my eldest sister-in-law did not get on at all, and although we lived in the same house, we cooked separately. It was there that I gave birth to my third daughter. At this, my mother-in-law insulted me and told my husband to take another wife. She refused to give me any food and said it was my fault for getting only daughters since we had had a love marriage. As we had saved a little money we decided to buy a house of our own and live there. Two years later, my son was born. Now my mother-in-law is living with us again as her second son threw her out about ten years ago.

Working as a Midwife in Thimi

Once it was known in the neighbourhood that I had been trained as a midwife, women started to ask me to help with pre-natal care and deliveries. They are aware that the traditional midwives don't know the full facts about pregnancy and also, that they (the midwives) themselves sometimes ask for my help if they cannot handle a birth. However, I always advise the women to go for check-ups at the hospital as well.

I also still go for deliveries together with my mother-in-law; she does the spirit-healing part and I do the midwifery as I was taught during my training. I control the progress of the birth, boil the razor blade, cut the cord and clean the mother and baby with soap and warm water. Sometimes a woman of the lower *Kata* caste is called to cut the cord, but nowadays, the old tradition of placing the placenta in a pot rarely occurs. If there is a complication I send the woman to the hospital. I have been doing this work now for fourteen years and I help with about four deliveries a month. The families pay me one hundred rupees for a delivery, fifty for a check-up and five or ten rupees when they come to my house for advice.

In my opinion, this work is really important because one can save lives. Several years ago in this village many mothers and babies used to die. My mother-in-law lost seven sons and four daughters and has only three sons still alive. Before it was much worse, but now things have changed because midwives have been taught safer practices. For me the work is also good from the welfare point of view; apart from saving lives it is an important part of development in society. It is responsible work for which one needs great commitment.

The Ups and Downs of the Job

If I am called out at night I am really afraid to go out. Recently a woman was killed early in the morning when it was foggy. I also find it frustrating that the progress in midwifery is so slow. There are still midwives, especially the older ones, who are still delivering in dirty places, using unclean knives and who are not sending women with complications to the hospital. They just don't care about those women's lives or the pain they are suffering they care only about their own reputation. I try to explain to them about the dangers of the old practices but they don't listen and that makes me feel sad and depressed.

I feel so happy when everything is going smoothly during a delivery, with everything nicely

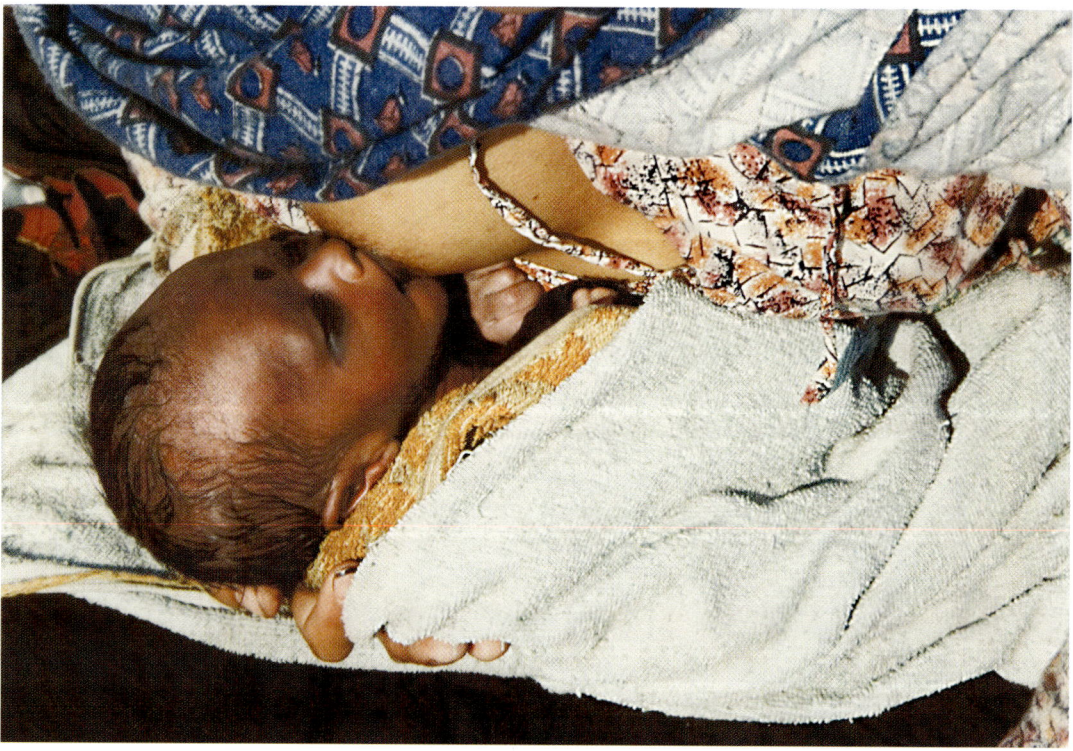

Rukmani checking a young mother and her newborn baby

Rukmani in the doorway during the initiation ritual of her nephews

cleaned with soap and when the parents get the boy or girl they wanted. What I still find difficult to accept is how people react when a girl is born. I believe that it is a wonderful thing when one gives birth to a new human being. If people are not happy about the gender of the child they should remain silent and shouldn't immediately shout out that they are disappointed. The mother can faint at that time and needs a while to recover before being confronted with the news. All the people are watching the mother only to see what gender the child will be but there is no concern about the pain the mother is going through.

Let me tell you the story of my friend next door. She gave birth to two sons but they both died and thereafter she gave birth to five daughters. Although she was already forty-six years old she wanted to try once more but again a daughter was born. Knowing how badly they wanted a son I quickly concealed the sex of the baby and only showed her the girl after a couple of hours. The mother started to cry, all the other daughters cried too and the father almost fainted. The whole household reacted as if someone had died! In the end the father turned to drink because he had no sons and he died of alcoholism some years later.

I try to convince mothers that it is not so bad to have a girl. I tell them that *Bhagawan* has given them the child and they have to accept that gift. I also tell them that it is better to have one good daughter who will take care of you in your old age than one hundred bad sons: these days daughters often take better care of their mothers than any of these long-awaited sons.

— *Eva Kipp and Marieke van Vliet*

Back to the Roots

Praja family in front of their house in Chhervang

2

June Maya Praja and Kausirani Praja

Back to the Roots

THE PRAJA OR Chepang people live in the central region of Nepal and are one of the country's aboriginal groups, their origins only recorded in legend and folklore. Originally, they lived a nomadic hunter-gatherer existence in dense forest and had virtually no contact with the outside world until about eighty years ago when they started to settle and cultivate their first crops on the steep, stony slopes of the low hills. Most burn a patch of forest and then cultivate, but as the harvest is only sufficient for about six months, families return to the forest to gather wild food plants for the rest of the year. The decreasing area of forest, however, is making it more difficult to find good food. During the lean months most of the men folk try to earn money as porters but their earnings are more often spent on alcohol than on food.

Other ethnic groups, usually through ignorance, regard the Praja as a very backward group with a low status in society. Although their socio-economic status may be low they have a distinctive and complicated social structure and are by nature peaceful and introspective, a trait that has caused them to be exploited by more aggressive neighbours. The authorities have tried several special development programmes for them in the village of Chhervang, in the hills of Chitwan district in Central Nepal, where a school was built. The Praja are animists and their festivals are linked to the lunar cycles. In the past all dead were buried, contrary to Hindu tradition, but cremation is also practiced nowadays.

There is no discrimination between boys and girls in their society, however, virtually all women are illiterate and only a few of the men have been to school for a short period. The health situation is not good, especially for women who lose on average forty-six per cent of their children. Few women go to the health post for vaccinations and usually give birth alone outside

Praja mother and her daughter

Praja girl watching her little sister

the house. The society accepts both arranged and love marriages and some couples elope. Most women receive a gift of a *chiuri* tree or cattle from their parents when they get married and these things remain their property, often serving as a kind of insurance in bad times when there is illness or when a house burns down.

June Maya Praja

June Maya is thirty-five years old and for most of the year lives with her five children and parents-in-law in a tiny house at the top of a very steep hill in the poorest part of Chhervang village. For part of the year the family moves to a shack near their cultivated land to protect the crops from monkeys. June Maya seems to be constantly busy, her hands never at rest and while talking with us she peels wild roots for a snack and enjoys the occasional hand-rolled cigarette. Her demeanour does not seem to reflect the misfortune she has suffered during her life.

When we arrived at her house in the morning her two elder boys had already left for school. Only a quarter of the children in the village attend school and June Maya has made considerable sacrifices so that they can go, even to the extent of doing the work the boys would otherwise have done. She is hopeful, however, that they will go on to get good jobs later on, maybe as teachers, or at least will be able to calculate prices in the market after finishing their education. She is usually the first in the village to go to the forest to gather food every morning and, after talking with us she leaves for the forest, singing, along with her husband.

June Maya Reminisces

The Early Years
I remember when I was a child I used to spend a lot of time playing either with stones or on the huge swing that people in the village had made. I used to sing a lot and even now I still like to make up my own songs. I had to help my mother to do the cooking and collect firewood but sometimes, if I couldn't be bothered to help her, she would shout at me and call me bad names which made me very upset. There was always enough to eat in our family even though there were quite a few of us. At one time I had nine brothers and sisters but seven of them died. I don't actually remember them dying as I was still very young. I myself was very ill when I was about five years old. My grandmother told me later that I hadn't eaten for sixteen days and almost died

June Maya Praja cutting wild roots or *gitas*

too. I was not afraid however, as I was very small and did not really understand about death at that age.

When I was thirteen years old I fell in love. I started to think about eloping. We have a song about this (singing):

> *If I elope with my loved one,*
> *I will be the butt of much gossip,*
> *I fear the bad tongues,*
> *But if I do not elope,*
> *My youth will be wasted.*

My parents agreed with my choice of husband, organised an official marriage and gave me a *chiuri* tree as a wedding present. In the beginning I was quite scared when my in-laws became angry with me and called me names. When your own parents do that you know that they love you anyway, but with your husband's parents it is different. Shortly after I got married my three-year-old sister died and I remember crying so much I thought I would never be able to stop. However, later in life I was also to lose two children myself. I was also very sad when my father expired three years ago. He was ill and was taken to the hospital in Bharatpur for treatment, but thirteen days later he died. Nobody was with him at the time and the news of his death reached our family three days afterwards. Upon hearing the news from my brother I felt devastated and cried. I remember wondering whether I was the only one who had ever felt such sorrow.

My brothers collected the body and buried it near the river in Narayanghat. I stayed in my own house and after twelve days went to my mother's house to do the purification rites which meant sprinkling 'goldwater' and cow's urine over everything in the house. To make this 'goldwater' we had to place a piece of gold jewellery in a pitcher of water for a short time to purify the water. Once the ritual of purification was completed we could cook and serve food to all the guests who had come to pay their last respects. Some time later my mother married again.

In our society when someone is ill we go to the *pande* who also conducts the ceremony after children are born. When I had given birth to my children he consulted the gods and gave the kids their names. We also believe in witches. Lan, the jungle witch, bit one of my daughters and she became very ill with pains in her stomach. That particular daughter had a weak spirit which is why it happened to her and not to my other children.

Constant Hard Work

My life is one of constant hard work. At least my mother-in-law helps with the cooking and my sons sometimes help me to get fodder but most of the time I work alone. We have many problems with our land and can usually only manage to produce enough food for five months. Last year part of the land was destroyed by a landslide, and a combination of the wind and marauding troops of monkeys ruined the harvest, so now we stay in a shack right next to the land for part of the year so we can see exactly what is going on.

I also spend a lot of time collecting roots from the forest and this year I have already started gathering in February. Nowadays, I have to go really deep in the forest to find these roots and it takes me a whole day to collect one basketful which provides us with enough food for four days. Sometimes my husband helps with this collection but I also go there with friends, in which case we sing and have a lot of fun together, the same as when we help each other with the maize harvest. I always sing while I'm gathering food in the jungle and this is one of my favourite songs:

> *There is a bundle of worries in this place,*
> *And if I want to put it down,*
> *There is no resting place wherever I look.*

Collecting roots is not easy. First you have to recognise where they are by the small, thin branches sticking out of the ground and then you must dig, which is the hardest part. Sometimes you dig down really deep only to discover that the mice have got there before you. I cook the roots or *gitas* beside a well in the forest not far from the house. It is far easier near a plentiful

June Maya and her family eating *gitas*

source of water as you need such a lot in which to wash and cook them. First I cut the roots into slices and then boil them in a mixture of water and ashes to make them taste less bitter. *Tarul* or yam is the most delicious root but it has become difficult to find nowadays.

For the rest of the year we eat maize or millet porridge. We always try to eat twice a day and if there is not enough money for us to do this, we sell goats or take a loan from the shopkeeper. I always look forward to the festival of *Dashain*, as we eat special foods like rice and meat at that time; it is my favourite time of the year and I do not mind collecting the firewood when I know it is for cooking a really delicious meal.

Men get a Better Deal

As far as possessions are concerned, my property consists of my clothes, two pans, two tin cans and a few spoons. I also have the *chiuri* tree that my parents gave me, one goat and six chickens. I had a few more chickens but a hawk swooped down and carried off three of them in one go. If I take the *chiuri* seeds to the market myself then the money I get from selling them is my own, and with that money I can buy whatever I like. If there is enough, I usually buy clothes for my children and myself. I also occasionally make and sell *jaand*, a kind of local beer. I find that if I go to the market with a group of women friends it is far more difficult to bargain for a fair price. Women just have to accept whatever the shopkeeper will pay, whereas men always manage to get a better deal. Therefore, I don't sell our lentils and maize unless my husband and I go together.

In the run up to the election all sorts of people visited our homes making speeches full of promises. We let them talk but it was the men from the village who told us what we had to do. They told us there were several boxes with different drawings such as a sun and a tree and we had to put the paper in the box with the tree. However, the old people didn't understand that and just threw their papers away.

I am not looking forward to the time when I will be old. My son and daughter-in-law will have to take care of me then and they might become irritated with me and not treat me well. I personally feel that if I work really hard now I might have fewer problems later on; it is far better if you can remain independent and determine your own future.

Kausirani Praja

The first time we meet Kausirani she says laughingly, 'My name means "queen" but I am not in the least like a queen if you see what has happened in my life.' She is forty-five years old and lives in a wooden house with her husband and his second wife; her co-wife has five children but Kausirani has none of her own. For various reasons she is an exceptional woman in Chhervang; she is one of two women in the village who tried to learn how to read and write despite the lack of school facilities in those days. Still convinced of the value of literacy, she actively encourages her co-wife's children to attend school now. She is also one of the only women in Chhervang who owns an area of lowland for rice cultivation.

At the time when we visit Kausirani she is worried. She has had trouble with her health and someone else has started to use her precious lowland, so she has had to go to court several times over her property rights. She gives answers to our questions in a very careful way and seems to think deeply about what has happened both in her own life and in the village. It becomes clear to us why the village chairman asked her to start a women's group to protect the local forest.

Kausirani Praja

25

Kausirani Praja Tells Her Life Story

Goats and Tigers

I remember talking, laughing, even fighting a lot with my friends when I was young. We used to shoot things by putting a *tata* seed in a hollow stick, and we would climb trees and swing in them. I had to help collect fodder and water, as well as looking after the family goats. But sometimes I would get fed up doing this every day and I would escape. That made my mother very angry, as she was when I lost our goats. I was out tending the goats with my friends and we decided to gather everyone's goats together in one big herd. Some goats stayed behind, and when it was time to go home again I couldn't find our animals, there were just too many. I was very afraid of going home, but luckily they all returned home on their own later that evening. Sometimes when we were tending the goats in the forest we would see a tiger. We always knew when a tiger was approaching, as the goats would become nervous and then we would run away as fast as possible.

Once when I was small, I saw someone writing a letter. I was fascinated and decided I would like to be able to do that too. I thought that if I had the chance to study, maybe I could become somebody important. Some time later, I went to the hospital in Bharatpur where I saw nurses and teachers and again I wondered whether I could learn to do that sort of job. I was disappointed that I could not learn to read and write as there was no local school at that time and, besides, I had to help with the household chores.

Early Marriage

At the age of eleven my parents arranged my marriage with a eighteen-year old boy. The boy's parents came to our house with rice, pigs and alcohol and the following day we all went over to the house of my in-laws, my parents bearing similar gifts. My parents gave me two chickens and six goats as a marriage present. Only a year later my mother died and was buried in the forest. As men always bury the dead I did not see her body. The men dig a hole, put in some wood and then the body, more wood, and then fill in the rest with earth. On top of the grave they place a few pots and pans as the dead might need them. After the daughters have purified the house, those men who carried the body to the grave and other guests are invited to eat at the house. Until the fifth day the spirit of the deceased can come back to the house. The spirit sometimes just stands in the doorway or can be heard drawing water from the pot, and if this should happen, we call the *pande* to help us send the spirit on its way.

The Literacy Class

When I was fourteen years old my in-laws sent me to a literacy class. The villagers paid two rupees each to the teacher, a Magar, who used to do a small *puja* to Saraswati, the goddess of knowledge, before the class started. We started with sixteen women and seventeen men, most of whom were married; there was even a fifty-year old woman in the class. Many dropped out in the first few weeks and after six months the class stopped when the teacher disappeared. We sometimes talked about starting a class again but it never happened. It was my father-in-law who was so keen that I should be able to read and write but I was only able to attend classes for one month as my mother-in-law died and I then had to take over her work. Later on friends taught me to read and write.

Another Wife

After several years of marriage we still hadn't any children and I wished that my husband would take me to the hospital so we could find out why. However, my husband then fell in love with another woman and decided to take a second wife. From that moment, I realised I would have to live without children of my own and would suffer for that. It was not an easy time getting used to a co-wife being around, but I never thought of running away as I was only twenty years old and not really aware of much at that stage. Nowadays, even though we work together quite well, there is still something between us. It is like a new cloth that gets dirt on it, you wash it but it always remains dirty — it can never really become clean ever again.

My Dreams

I always dream a lot. Sometimes my dreams are auspicious ones about milk, which mean that we will get some money, and ones about crossing a river or walking uphill are also good. Last night I dreamt that I was walking downhill. Some people were building a wall and told me to go down but I said I wanted to go up, and I did, so the dream was good after all. I have bad dreams quite often and these make me very ill. In such dreams maybe I am travelling alone and once I dreamt I was in a big house where officials were writing in registers. They told me to stay there and I was very scared.

After that particular dream I became very sleepy all the time and had a fever, so I consulted the *pande*. He told me that the god 'Babi', who determines our life and future, had taken my spirit and that I should conduct a *puja* for him or else I might die. I had to prepare a cord from nine threads and put nine knots in it representing the nine planets. Then I had to offer the god a plate of rice, money and a goat as a sacrifice.

The *pande* came in the evening to perform the ceremony. First, he talked to his drum and then he called the local gods, 'Simebhume' and 'Thani', and then his personal god, 'Phola'. When 'Phola' touches the *pande*, he shakes all over. He describes it as being similar to being splashed with cold water. I had to sit in front of the *pande* who put leaves on the goat and moved it around behind my back, asking 'Babi' whether he would accept the goat as a sacrifice and

Kausirani during here treatment by the shaman or *pande*

leave my spirit alone. He then spoke for a long time with all the gods while beating his drum and, finally, the goat was slaughtered.

A Special Piece of Land

I saved the money that I got from selling some of my own goats and bought a pair of golden earrings. Later my father-in-law sold all my animals and in return gave me a patch of lowland on which to cultivate rice, a rare commodity in this area. However, about a year ago somebody else started to work on my land and took the harvest for himself. That land is in my name and now I have to keep going to court to fight for my rights, as the man continues to usurp my land. I am so worried that I will lose that land as, besides the two chickens and six goats, that is all I have in the world. Sadly, my father-in-law died some years ago and I really wish that he was here now to help me defend my rights to the land.

Change

Things have changed a lot since I was young. Some of our festivals are no longer celebrated such as *Namrung*, a big ceremony performed by men in the forest for the god of hunting, but we still do the *Buimi* ceremony in January. Once every five years we sacrifice a buffalo, and a goat in the other four. The men do everything, even the cooking, while the women watch. Lately the size of the festival is far smaller than in previous years.

In my childhood there were only twelve houses in Chhervang, all with roofs made of leaves. In those days food was plentiful. There was forest all around and tigers would come near the houses. Our villagers burned the wood to claim more land to farm and gradually the hills became barren, the terraces started to collapse and there were landslides whenever it rained. People cut trees to sell them, and this must be stopped. The ward chairman has asked me to form a group of women to guard the forest, and we want to do something about the water problem too. Up to now, Chhervang is the only village in this area where there has been no development work done at all.

I am not sure if the children of my co-wife will help me when I get old. These days I am not so strong as before and cannot do a lot of heavy work and old people become ill so easily. I imagine my later life as being a difficult time full of worry and uncertainty.

Kausirani's Favourite Story

The Little Voice from the Earth

A long time ago, in a small house near the forest there lived two brothers, Kyanglang and Changlang Dang. Changlang was still very young so his elder brother gave him easy work to do. While Kyanglang did the heavy work in the fields Changlang went off gathering wild yams. Once, while he was busy digging up yams, he heard a human voice that seemed to come from the ground. It was the voice of a girl. The voice said, 'Your name is Changlang Dang and my name is Chanbhari. We are of the same age and are a good match. We should marry but don't tell this to your brother because if he knows he will kill me.'

After that Changlang heard the same girl's voice every time he went to dig yams. For some time Changlang didn't tell his brother anything, but eventually, he announced to Kyanglang that he wasn't going to go digging yams anymore. Kyanglang was surprised and asked him why he didn't want to go, so Changlang told him all about the little voice that came from the ground. He added, 'I am worried about her. She sounds so sweet. I love her voice but I don't know if she is a demon, a witch or a human being.' 'She must be a witch,' said Kyanglang, 'No human being lives under the ground. But don't be afraid, I'll go with you and hide myself nearby. Whenever she comes out I will kill her.'

Together, they went off to the jungle and as soon as Changlang started to dig he heard the same voice again. Changlang informed his brother and told him not to kill the girl if she looked nice. Just at that moment the girl came out of the ground for the first time. Without hesitation Kyanglang threw his poisoned spear at her. He wanted to kill her but he missed. Chanbhari was

29

very angry with them both. She told Changlang that she had wanted to marry him, but since they had tried to kill her marriage was out of the question. While saying this she slowly disappeared into the ground and vanished forever. Changlang was very upset. 'I told you not to kill her if she looked nice,' he shouted at his brother, 'but you tried to kill her anyway.'

As time went by, Changlang couldn't forgive his brother and he left their home to look for another place to live but Kyanglang followed his brother because he didn't want to live without him. Changlang eventually turned himself into a *guelo* tree so Kyanglang couldn't find him anymore. One day Kyanglang grew very weary and leaned against the tree near him but, as he did so, he felt the tree swaying and realised that his brother had changed himself into the tree. He then changed himself into a big *chirolo* tree not far from the *guelo* tree and for many years they continued to live very close together.

— *Eva Kipp*

Artists' Impressions

Maithili paintings on the walls of the houses near Janakpur

Maithili wall painting

3

Anuragi Devi Jha and Hira Karna
Artists' Impressions

THE PLAINS IN the south-east of Nepal were once part of the ancient and powerful Hindu Kingdom of Mithila which also encompassed parts of present-day India. The people of this kingdom had their own language — Maithili, which is still spoken in some eight districts of Nepal as well as in the Indian states of Bihar and West Bengal. The town of Janakpur was formerly the capital of Mithila, and to this day pilgrims from both India and Nepal come to worship at the Janaki temple, which is dedicated to goddess Sita. Many Hindu legends have their origin in this area. According to the famous Asian epic *Ramayana*, Ram and Sita, the ideal king and queen of Vedic culture, were married in this town.

Maithili culture has a rich heritage of literature and art and the themes and details of the local paintings, which are made by women, vary from caste to caste. Women in the Brahmin and Kayastha castes, traditionally the priests and administrators in Hindu society, mostly depict Hindu gods and goddesses and their incarnations. The paintings are done on the outer walls of the local mud houses and they play an important role in religious festivals and rituals.

Traditionally, the freedom of Maithili women has been highly restricted. High caste Maithili women live in strict seclusion because of the great value attached to sexual purity; it is considered prestigious for the family if their women do not have to work outside the home. Girls are not allowed to play with boys, and young women are obliged to hide their faces with a veil, both from older men in their family and male outsiders in general. Women are not supposed to raise their voices, and it is said that the voice of a young woman should not be heard by men other than her husband and his younger brothers. So communications to others are often passed through children.

The rigidity of Maithili society is, however, gradually changing. It is now more than two decades since roads were built connecting Kathmandu with the southern plains. Malaria has been eradicated from the Maithili areas. Maithili culture has had to embrace many modern influences, and many activities in the field of education and development have altered women's perception of their position in society and of their potential. However, the transformation of their traditional art into more marketable forms has had a most important effect as well. One recent project, which has had a significant impact on the lives of individual Maithili women, is the Janakpur Women's Development Centre where the traditional Maithili art has been revived for the production of paintings and products which can be sold in Kathmandu and abroad. The women have learned how to transfer the traditional design and techniques to other art forms such as sewing, weaving, printing and ceramics. They are now able to leave the seclusion of their homes and travel from their villages to Janakpur and other cities in Nepal where they have earned money and respect through their paintings and designs.

Anuragi Devi Jha

When we first meet Anuragi Jha she is busy doing a painting on the wall of the Summit hotel in Kathmandu. It is a colourful Lord Shiva riding an elephant. She is working together with a younger colleague Hira Karna and it is obvious that they are enjoying themselves. Anuragi likes to tease the younger woman: 'Where are the birds in your trees?', 'What is that dog doing there?', and 'Give him a red pepper to eat!' When the two artists add the male organs to a rather skinny dog, they break into uncontrollable giggles. Anuragi is a thin woman with a lively, some-what mischievous expression. She is dressed in a simple yellow sari, and on her forehead she wears a *tika* of red powder.

Anuragi is from the Brahmin caste and adheres strictly to religious customs. She fasts every month on the day of the full moon, and keeps her own shrine in the house of her son-in-law in Janakpur. In addition to daily worship inside the house she also pays a visit to all the main temples in Janakpur every day, taking a plate with flowers and food as an offering to the gods and once a month she requests a Brahmin priest to perform a ceremony for her family during which he reads the holy books while Anuragi offers the gods food, flowers, candles and incense.

Anuragi Devi Jha

Anuragi doing a wall painting of Lord Shiva riding an elephant

We go to Kumhaura, where Anuragi lives, to visit her in her own surroundings. As we approach her home the local women hurriedly veil their faces and scurry in all directions to their houses. A moment later when her father-in-law appears Anuragi and her daughter-in-law bow down and touch his feet with their foreheads. Anuragi tells us that this is how Maithili women show respect, which is reflected in the proverb: 'If the wife is obedient, disciplined and nice, the husband can sleep soundly and sweetly.' Little has changed regarding the traditional superiority of men.

When Anuragi speaks, her wrinkled face livens up and seems to tell its own life story. Talking quickly and making gestures with her head and hands to express her emotions, Anuragi tells us about her life as the wife of a high caste Maithili farmer.

Anuragi's Story
Childhood
I am Anuragi Devi Jha. I am about sixty years old and was born in the village of Kaluwahi in the state of Bihar, India, where my father used to work as a farmer. I have three elder brothers and a sister. When I was young I used to help my mother with washing the dishes and taking lunch to my father and brothers whenever they were working in the fields. Our house was made of mud and had a thatched roof. My grandmother, mother and sister used to paint the walls and courtyard with a mixture of red and yellow clay, cow-dung and rice flour. They made decorations showing birds, gods and goddesses and whenever there was a wedding or a full moon festival they used to do a particularly beautiful and elegant floor-painting known as 'Aripana'. From a very early age I copied what the other women in the house were doing, trying out different ways of mud painting and inventing my own designs. That is how I learned to paint.

In those days Maithili girls, and especially those from the Brahmin caste, were not sent to school. Like the other villagers, my parents thought that a girl could lose her purity by playing with boys and studying in mixed classes. As a child I thought that I would grow up to have the same sort of life as my mother. I knew nothing about marriage then. Once, when I was about eleven years old, I was crying because I was hungry, but when I asked my father for rice he did not have any and said instead that he would try to find a Nepali boy for me. I thought he had just said that to make me stop crying, so I paid no attention to his words as I thought it had little to do with me being hungry. However, my father did indeed arrange my marriage shortly afterwards and within a few days I was sent to my new home.

Only much later did I understand, that according to ancient rites and rituals in our community, people arrange the marriage of a daughter before her first menstruation. There is a big mango tree in the village, which we call 'Loha', where unmarried boys are taken in order to arrange their marriage. This tradition, known as *saurath*, takes place in the summer months of

Anuragi touching the feet of her father-in-law

June and July and it was here, under the mango tree, that my father chose a husband for me; the boy was just thirteen years old.

The Duties of a Daughter-in-Law

When I was sent to my new home in Nepal, my parents put me in a sedan chair. I was wearing a long, red, uncomfortable sari and bangles — these were not the modern glass bangles but lacquered ones we call *lahati*. I carried a small tin box containing my belongings. That was all I brought along. Since I did not understand what was happening, I concluded that my parents had sold me and this made me so upset that all I could do was cry and cry all the way to the new house.

At the time of my marriage I knew nothing about the duties of a daughter-in-law. I had no idea how to treat a husband either, so I simply regarded him as a friend. It was the unhappiest period of my life, and I hope no other woman will have to suffer like I suffered then. I repeatedly implored my in-laws to take me back to my family but they always replied that I was now living in my 'uncle's house' and should stay just a few days more. However, time passed and they did not take me back. Several women from the neighbourhood started to visit me and they told me how I should behave and how to go about my work. Only after two years did I finally understand that I was a daughter-in-law and realise what my duties were.

After that I started to wear a veil. I used to massage my mother-in-law every night and comb and plait the hair of my younger sisters-in-law. Before sleeping I was supposed to 'amuse' my husband. I had to get up very early to wash the dishes and do the cooking. Every morning I had to bow down before my husband and touch his feet with my forehead as a sign of my respect; then I had to wash his feet in a bowl of water and drink some of the dirty water afterwards.

When I had finished cooking the morning meal I would first serve my father-in-law, my brother-in-law and my husband and only when they had finished could I serve the women. I was only allowed to have my meal once everyone else had eaten and I was expected to eat from my husband's uncleaned plate. I was not allowed to speak to the men or older people in the house. If I wanted to say something to them I had to pass a message through the younger men in the family. I was not allowed to leave the house alone but occasionally went outside together with my mother-in-law who was very kind to me.

Education

Some time later we moved to our own house in Kumhaura, about 9 km from Janakpur, where we had a small piece of land and some cattle. My husband is illiterate but he is a very generous man. He is a farmer so he looks after our cattle and earns a little money by selling milk but these earnings were never enough to send our children to school. A few times during my journeys from my home to Janakpur or to my parental home in India, I saw how other people were improving their economic status by going to school. When a literacy class started near our house I decided to go, too. Today I am still barely literate but I can read a little and I am able to write my name. Throughout my life I have found this lack of literacy very difficult and I decided I did not want to see my children suffer that way.

When I saw that our neighbours were sending their children to school I started to wonder how I could send mine too. My parents invited my eldest son to live with them in India so he could study over there, which was a big help, but there were still three children left who did not go to school. I decided to take a small loan from the neighbours and started a tiny teashop in one of the rooms of our house. At first, my in-laws disapproved of the idea but, nowadays, it seems they are happy that I started the shop.

Apart from tea and snacks I also started to sell *paan*, *betel* nut, soap and other things too. Elderly villagers were very critical and teased me for being a shopkeeper but my husband supported me; he knew that we needed the money for the children's schooling and started to bring goods for the shop from Janakpur. Although I was a shopkeeper, I was still not allowed to show my face to most of the customers, so I sat in an adjoining inside room and gave instructions to my children as to what to do and how to serve the customers. From the earnings I was able to send my sons and daughter to school and even save some money. I was very proud of this and it showed me that there is no real difference between women and men — both are equally capable of earning money.

Due to these efforts my sons have completed their studies and now have good jobs. My first son works as an administrator in a childcare centre, the second is a teacher and the third an overseer. For people with an education things have changed a lot. Nowadays, even women do voluntary development work. They go from door to door motivating women to come to literacy classes and also teach local women about eating good food during pregnancy and about safe childbirth.

Women and Work

In my opinion, women who always have to stay inside the house lead a fairly meaningless life. My life has now changed completely since five years ago when I heard about the Janakpur Art Centre. My husband, like others in the village, was not particularly enthusiastic about it at first. The general opinion was that a project in which foreigners were involved would have a bad influence on the women. The Centre accepted me because of my painting skills. Because I had been confined to the house for so many years, I had had lots of time to improve my painting.

I am now a project employee at the Centre and I earn 1,600 rupees per month. We elect the most suitable women to be members of a committee, which then decides on the formats and guidelines for our paintings. We mostly paint traditional religious designs but we also include scenes from daily life, things that happen in the village and paintings about the position of Maithili women in society. I am free to use my imagination when designing and the project gives us further training and provides us with painting materials. Foreigners buy most of our work but many Nepali offices and institutions, such as the university, ask us to do wall paintings for them.

Since starting to work in Janakpur I have learned a lot. Before I started work I was afraid of travelling to Janakpur on my own. How to get to a place, how to talk to other people, and what others might say about me were things I used to worry about, but nowadays I don't even hesitate to talk to people whom I don't know. While travelling for the project I have met so many different kinds of people and this has enabled me to look at the world and my life in a very different way. I can now wear nice clothes and no longer need to ask others for money, in fact I am even saving money for the future. I feel that this is the happiest time of my life. I finally feel as if I am not shut away in prison any more.

Hira Karna

Hira Karna, a young, slightly plump Maithili woman, lives with her two sons in a tiny mud house in Nagarain, some 12 km from Janakpur. Her single-room home is part of a group of traditional houses built around a courtyard where Hira's relatives have settled. A tall bamboo pole marks the ceremonial places used by the family and Hira proudly shows us the *kobar* which is a room in the bride's house where the newly-married couple spend their first nights together. The room is decorated with an ornate tantric design also called *kobar*. The outside walls of the houses are freshly coated with a plain mixture of cow-dung and mud, and the colourful Maithili paintings which used to adorn these walls can no longer be seen.

Hira takes the bus every day from her village to Janakpur to work at the Art Centre. 'When I travel I don't talk to anyone because people might think badly of me,' she says. Hira's life changed dramatically when her husband took a second wife and stopped supporting her and their two sons. She was forced to take some courageous decisions that enabled her to live an independent life. Due to being badly treated by her husband, the young artist is now quite outspoken about the suffering in her life, caused both by traditional norms and the attitude of her husband.

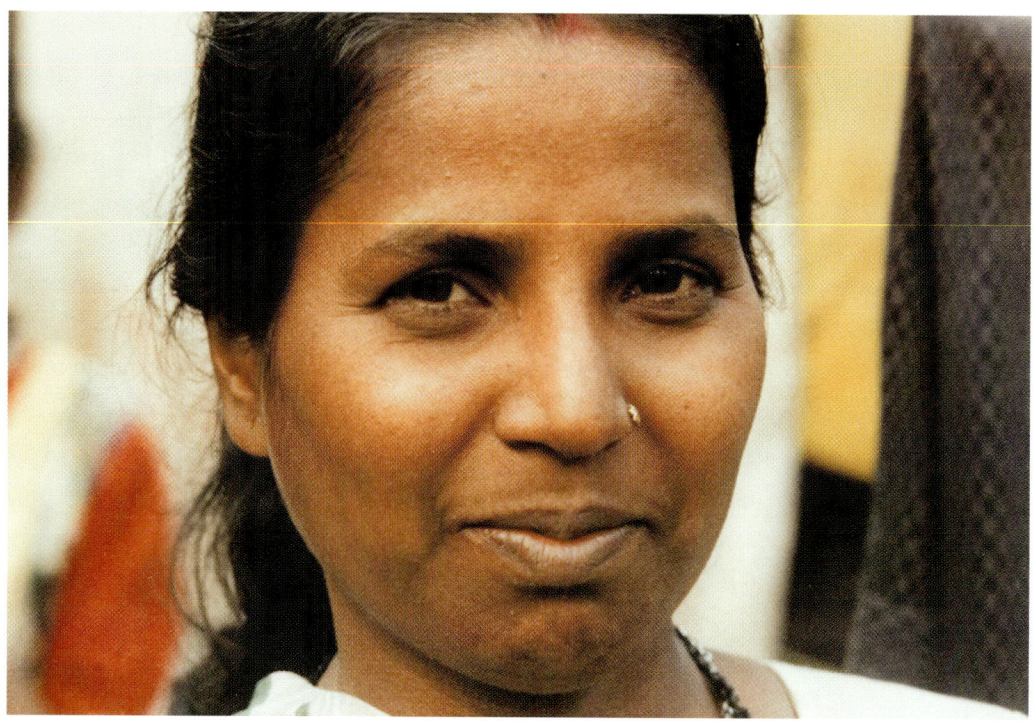
Hira Karna

Thoughtful but determined, Hira talks about her life and her eyes light up when she describes the painting and the travelling she does for her work. When we reach her home she continues to talk about her life and her eyes fill with tears when she tells us about the period when she had to return to her parental home. If the topic of marriage comes up she declares that she would never, ever go through that again.

Hira Karna Tells Her Life Story

Early Life and Marriage

My name is Hira Karna — the surname is my *own*, not that of my husband. I belong to the *Kayastha* caste and I was born in Nagarain, about twenty-five years ago. My father was a teacher at the lower secondary school and I have three brothers and two sisters. My eldest brother is now employed in the sugar factory in Butwal and my younger brother has just passed his School Leaving Certificate examination. Both my sisters are married.

I spent my childhood inside the house doing the work that women are supposed to do but I also liked to help my mother make the traditional Maithili paintings in the house. When we had some free time we used to tell stories and sing, and in the autumn we would play a game called *Shyama Chakheba* with mud figures. This is based on a story about a girl who was turned into a bird and later helped to change back into human form by her brother. For fourteen nights my friends and I would sing the story and then on the last evening of the full moon festival we would throw the mud figures into the pond. My grandmother was the best storyteller of all and one of my favourites was the one about the sun god, *Surya Bhagawan*.

I was sixteen when my marriage was arranged. My father had chosen one of the boys from our village as my bridegroom. Once I knew I was getting married I started to worry: I wondered what kind of person he would be, how he would treat me and what exactly I would have to do after the wedding. I only saw my husband when I went to his home after the wedding had taken place and I found out that he was seventeen years old, from our caste and had passed the School Leaving Certificate examination.

After the wedding ceremony I was put in a carriage and I remember weeping bitterly because I did not want to leave my parents' home. In my husband's house I had to get up well before sunrise to start the daily household chores such as washing dishes and clothes, cooking the meals, cleaning and decorating the house and pounding grains like rice and maize. During various festivals I often had to wash my husband's feet and drink some of the water. On other days, I just bowed and touched his feet with my head. Before going to sleep I was supposed to give a massage both to my mother-in-law and my husband and another daily chore was to comb the hair of my sisters-in-law. I never got the chance to leave the house and even inside I had to cover my head and face with my sari or shawl in front of my husband's parents, elder brothers and, sometimes, even my husband. When I wanted to say something to men older than me, I had to ask a younger relative to do so. My mother-in-law was always asking me to do all sorts of things and if I did not do them fast enough she would get angry.

My husband was able to earn a little money as a clerk in an office which dealt with land revenue. We did not have enough land to support the family but, generally, I didn't really have a bad time with my in-laws. After four years of marriage our first son was born. During the delivery and for several days afterwards I had to stay in a dirty room and I was not allowed to eat rice or green vegetables, just a kind of porridge called *haluwa* and some medicine made out of ginger. During that period my husband's family called a *rady*, a person from an untouchable caste, who massages the mother and the baby with mustard oil twice a day. On the sixth day, which we call *chathiyaar*, a barber came, cut our nails and bathed both of us in an act of ritual purification. The baby and I could then wear new clothes and the family cooked delicious food for the many guests who were invited for this occasion.

Bad Times

Four years later when I gave birth to a second son, my husband brought home a second wife and my life took a turn for the worse. He starting treating me like a servant and gradually everybody in the house started to oppress me. Nobody ever gave me any money, neither for clothes, nor even for medicine when my boys were ill. Often I got no food at all. To this day I cannot understand why my husband treated me like this after I had given him two sons.

When my father saw my wretched existence he decided to take me home. That is how I, a married woman, went back to live in my parents' house where they have given me all the love and sympathy that I should have received from my husband. I also decided to get sterilised as my husband still occasionally spends the night with me; it is already difficult enough to support two children on my own and, besides, I am sure that I will never, ever marry again. After all, why should I?

At that time my life was miserable — I just cried and cried. When my son asked for clothes I had no money to buy any. When a literacy class was organised nearby I learned to read and write and I started to help my mother to paint the house, as I had done in my childhood, with cow-dung and lime. During festivals and weddings we would make pictures of gods, goddesses, elephants and birds all over the walls.

A Change for the Better

One day a foreigner called Miss Claire came to our village to look at the paintings. She invited me to come to the Janakpur Art Centre to work there as a painter and since then my life has changed tremendously. In the past I was too scared to even put a foot outside the house but now I can go all the way to Kathmandu on my own! I can now talk freely about anything and I am no longer worried about what my husband says to me: I am proud that I can take care of my sons on my own.

I work very hard nowadays; before I go off to Janakpur I have to do the cooking and then I come back at seven in the evening and take care of my sons. I don't have any leisure time but I am extremely happy and satisfied, even though the income is not really enough for supporting the family and giving them a good education. I feel that the lives of the many women who are rejected by their husbands would improve if there were more projects like the one I am working with. If there had been good education and awareness programmes when I was a child, I might not have lived in poverty. I could have stood on my own two feet from the very beginning and could even have chosen my own husband! Life could have been a happy one, I guess.

Hira Tells a Maithili Folk Tale

Once, just before the August full moon appeared, it rained and continued raining for many days. For a long time the sun did not appear at all and women started to worry. They wanted to grind wheat and rice to make *daalpuri*, a kind of pancake made from flour, to offer to the moon during the festival of *Chauddhan* but without sunshine the wheat and rice would not dry. The women started to get desperate.

An old widow decided to do something about the situation and while worshipping the sun god she asked, 'Oh, dear sun god, if you give us the sunlight to dry the grains I will allow you to marry my only daughter.' Hearing the old widow's request the sun became very happy and immediately started to shine brightly. All the housewives thanked the sun god and ran to the widow's courtyard, which was the brightest place in the village, to dry their grains, and the *Chauddhan* festival of that year became the best one ever celebrated.

When the festivities came to an end, the sun god disguised himself as a man and went to the widow's house, hoping she would keep her promise. However, the widow, seeing the sun god approaching her house, quickly hid her daughter in a neighbour's house. The sun god returned many times, once even just before sunset, but every time the widow hid her daughter from him. When he found the house empty yet again, the sun god became extremely angry and urinated on the vegetables in the kitchen garden in front of the house.

After the widow and her daughter returned home, the daughter picked a green leaf from the garden and ate it unwashed. After eating the raw leaf she became pregnant and the news of her pregnancy spread throughout the village. Time passed and one day the daughter gave birth to a handsome son. The boy was teased a lot because he had no father. So, eventually, the son asked his mother who his father was. She told him the whole story and told the boy to bow to the sun. The boy bowed before the sun and, to his surprise the sun god came down to him and said, 'I will call you Curbut Bahan. Do not worry, just call the villagers for a meeting tomorrow.'

Next day, when all the villagers had gathered, a voice suddenly came from the sky, saying, 'Look at this boy. He is my son and you should all love him. Those of you who will fast and worship me every year will have a long and prosperous life.' From that day onwards most women on the Terai have celebrated the festival of *Kharatiya Pawani* by fasting and worshipping the sun god once a year.

— *Eva Kipp*

A Struggle to Survive

4

Khedani Devi Harijan
A Struggle to Survive

 PALHI VILLAGE IS situated close to the Indian border on the low-lying Terai, a narrow belt along the southern edge of Nepal which has a sub-tropical climate of hot, dry summers and cool winters. The area around Palhi is fairly typical for the Terai: the land has long since been under cultivation and very few trees now remain. Most of the original dense forest was cut down long ago when large numbers of people, from the hills to the north and from India to the south, migrated to the area and cleared the land in order to cultivate their crops.

Harijans form the largest ethnic group in Palhi; they are low caste, so-called 'untouchable' people, originating from India and traditionally engaged in unenviable or menial work such as sweeping, cleaning latrines and the disposal of carcasses. The name 'Harijan', meaning 'children of God', was given by Mahatma Gandhi in an attempt to give low caste people a better standing within society. Harijans in Palhi speak the 'Bhojpuri' language but some of the men also speak Nepali. They follow the Hindu religion and the festivals they celebrate tend to be more Indian than Nepali.

Most of them occupy very small parcels of land, which are too small to produce enough food to be self-sufficient. Their position is comparable with that of those who are completely landless — their land is not registered and they cannot claim any rights. For additional income they are dependent on the landlords who live in the same area. These landlords are often accused of exploiting the difficult situation of the Harijans. For example, during the peak agricultural season the landlords will pay them a mere twenty rupees for one whole day's work in their fields.

The standard of living of the Harijans in Palhi is generally low. Houses are built in clusters and are simple constructions made of mud and bamboo, often decorated with paintings or mud sculptures and with a thatched roof. Inside, large handmade clay pots are used for storing grains. Beds consist of a wooden frame strung with ropes and there are a few essential cooking utensils. As firewood is a scarce commodity, cooking is usually done with cakes of cow-dung that have been dried in the sun, sometimes agricultural waste is also used, and if nothing else is available, firewood.

Services are gradually improving in Palhi. There is now a health post where basic medical treatment, medicines and vaccinations are provided. A non-governmental organisation, the Institute for Integrated Development Studies (IIDS), has started various development activities in the village and has improved access to credit facilities. Previously, people had to go to the local Agriculture Development Bank, which required collateral before a loan could be issued whereas IIDS does not ask for any collateral.

Khedani Devi Harijan

When we met Khedani for the first time in the spring of 1994 she was quite negative about her life and situation, but when we meet her again nine months later she is a little more positive. Khedani looks thin, maybe as a result of the periods in her life when she did not get sufficient food. Her skin is dark, a characteristic of many low caste people, and contrasts attractively with the brightly coloured sari she is wearing, the tail of which she uses to cover her head in accordance with the local custom for married women.

She shows few emotions but she can raise a smile even while recalling some of the more unhappy events in her life. Her attitude seems at the same time both fatalistic and bitter: 'I was poor in the past, I am poor now and I will be poor in the future, that's life. The rich will be rich and the poor will be poor.' On other occasions, such as when we talk about property, she reveals a good sense of humour and likes to laugh and joke.

Khedani Devi Tells Her Story

Family

My name is Khedani Devi Harijan. I think I'm about forty years old but I'm not sure about my exact age as it isn't that important for us. When children are young we know their age but as

Khedani Devi Harijan

(Photo by Marieke van Vliet)

they grow older we forget it; we'll only remember if they were born before or after an event. I live here in the village of Palhi with my husband and our four children. Our eldest daughter is about nineteen or twenty years old now; she's married with one small son and lives together with her husband and his family. Our youngest child is, maybe, four — No, I think she is about three years old!

We did have more children but we lost two sons. Our eldest son died when he was three years old because of diarrhoea. At that time there was no health post either in or near the village so we couldn't do anything to help him. The second son we lost when he was only twelve days old. There didn't seem to be anything wrong with him. I had woken up early in the morning to feed him and after that we had both fallen asleep again. When it was time to wake up, he was dead. Losing children is part of life here and most women in our village will have about seven children and expect to lose two of them. Many other women in our village have had the same experience as I have.

Although our village is rather poor, I'm very fond of it. The social life in the village is good, and the people are friendly. Whenever necessary, people always help each other. All the people living in this part of the village are low caste people, most of them Harijans, like us.

Hard Labour

Because we are poor we have a hard life. We have no land of our own, except this spot on which our house is built, so we need to buy all our food. At least my husband is strong and healthy so, usually, we can make both ends meet. During the peak agricultural season both of us go together with our children who are old enough (about twelve years old) to work for the land-lords. They need extra labour for the rice planting, weeding the fields and for the harvest. If we work for one day in the fields we get twenty rupees and a small meal, *roti*, with vegetables, in the afternoon. In the hot season, when planting out the rice, we have a break from twelve to two o'clock; otherwise we work the whole day. This kind of work is available for about four or five months in a year. As all landlords pay the same rate for our labour, there is no point in working for anyone in particular; all landlords are the same.

When there is no work available here my husband cycles down to India where he buys pota-toes or other vegetables. He usually buys seventy kilos at the most and then sells them in the villages in the hills behind Sunwal, to the north, where he can make a profit of about three to four rupees per kilo. When the price of vegetables goes up too much he goes off to the big town of Butwal for one or two weeks at a time and hires a rickshaw. It costs twenty-five rupees per day to hire one and on an average day he can earn a minimum of forty rupees, which is enough for food. He doesn't have to pay for accommodation, as he sleeps outside. On market days, which

Khedani harvesting in the field of a landlord
(Photo by Marieke van Vliet)

Khedani making a basket
(Photo by Marieke van Vliet)

are twice a week, he can earn up to 250 rupees, and sometimes if he is lucky, foreigners pay him extra! This is how we earn the money to buy our food.

When there is no paid work to be had in the fields I spend my time doing my housework. It's not that much really, cooking food for the family, cleaning the house, putting a fresh layer of mud and cow-dung on the floor and walls, washing clothes, collecting fodder for the buffaloes and making cow-dung patties to dry for fuel. There is usually enough time left to relax and enjoy sitting outside for a chat with the neighbours. I also like to make baskets, which make nice presents for weddings.

For cooking, I use the dried dung, agricultural waste or firewood. My husband collects the firewood in the hills behind Sunwal but it is not easy these days, as it is now strictly forbidden to collect wood and the police patrol the area. However, we sometimes do need some firewood for cooking our food, as the dung from our animals is only enough for four months of the year, besides, wood is easier to use and gives less smoke.

A History of Poverty

After they married, my parents-in-law left their village and came here to Palhi. I'm not really sure why they moved here but I do know that they were poor. When they came here, some people had left this place and they were able to take it over. They built a house themselves, and when they died my husband inherited both the land and the house. Besides this we have one female buffalo and her calf. We bought the buffalo when she was small from the money my husband had earned. When our second daughter, who is already married, leaves home to join her husband, she will take the calf with her.

Although we are still poor as a family, I think our children have had an easier youth than my own or that of my husband. My mother died when I was about six or seven years old during a measles epidemic, and then my father died two years later during an epidemic of cholera. While my parents were alive, my life was good. I had to do some household chores which I learned by watching my mother, and then took over when I became a little older. My mother was like all Nepali mothers — she would tell me what to do and, if I did it properly, she was happy. But if I did it the wrong way, she became angry, so next time I would do it properly. There would usually be enough time left to play with my friends. We mostly played with either stones or mud. For one game you had to put five small stones on the back of your hand then turn your hand over quickly and try to catch the stones.

My family was poor but I did not realise this until after both my parents died. I then understood the true meaning of poverty. We had a small piece of land which was not nearly enough to feed us, so my brother hired himself out to rich people for all kinds of work, earning either rice or money for his labour. I was responsible for all the household work and the care of my younger sister. Life was difficult; often there was not enough food but my brother tried to save as much money as possible so he could buy a small pig. When I was nine years old he was able to buy a pig and I took care of it and later on looked after the newborn piglets, as well.

When I was ten years old my marriage was arranged by my brother. I can remember it as being a happy day with especially good food — there was rice, *dal* and vegetables and even yoghurt. After the wedding, I went back home and only five years later did I leave my parental home to start life together with my husband. We call this *tilak*: children marry when they are young, then after the wedding ceremony, they go back home. Some years later the girls leave their parental home to join their husband and his family and at that time they bring some goods for the family — and, if their family can afford it, they bring cattle too.

The day I left home was quite a happy event for me. I did feel a little sad at leaving my brother and sister, as I loved them, but I had not really been happy with my life since both parents died and I looked forward to having my 'own' family. From home I took some clothes, some kitchen utensils and a calf, which my brother bought for me. The calf was my own property but I was not allowed to sell it, as that would be considered a great insult to my own family. Later the cow had two calves which were sold by my husband, and the money spent on household needs.

I never did meet my husband's parents as they had both died before I was married. My

Khedani and her daughters
(Photo by Marieke van Vliet)

husband has two younger sisters, both of whom are married and living elsewhere with their husbands and families. My husband was in exactly the same position as my brother — when his parents died he had to take care of his two younger sisters. I am happy with my husband — he is a good man. He works hard to provide us with food and clothes, he does not drink or gamble and he has never beaten me.

My husband and I are Hindu, like the other people in our village. I like to celebrate the festivals like the birthdays of Krishna and Ram, *Shiva Raatri*, *Naag Panchami*, the first day of the month of *Magh* and *Holi*. The festivals which we celebrate in our village are more Indian than Nepali. We do not pay a lot of attention to the celebration of *Dashain*. During *Holi*, a group is formed in the village, consisting of men and women, together they go to other villages to sing and dance. They will get some food or money. The songs deal with the problems and happiness in daily life or they sing religious songs. I like to sing and to dance, that is why I like *Holi* very much. But other festivals are also very nice, during *Shiva Raatri* there is a fair and I enjoy going there.

The Future

Things are not changing very much for us except in a few minor ways. Before the elections people from all the political parties came to our village. They promised to help us but nothing has changed. They promised a decent road and electricity; it still hasn't come, but even if we did have electricity we wouldn't be able to pay the bill! Politics is rather difficult; you don't really know who to vote for, but this time my husband and I, both voted for the Congress party.

Nowadays IIDS is running a programme in our village. We can save money in groups and we can take loans. The maximum loan we can take is 5,000 rupees; for this we do not need to provide any collateral and the interest rate is low. I also became a member of one of these women's groups and took a loan to buy a goat. I was very pleased with it and wanted to start selling goats on a larger scale, but unfortunately the goat died. Now I have nothing to sell and I still have to repay the loan. I think it is possible to repay, but it will be difficult and will probably take a long time. IIDS has also started a tree-planting scheme in a nearby village. This is a good idea as there are hardly any trees in this area and haven't been for many years. It would be good to have some forest nearby, as fodder collection is now such a difficult job.

I don't know what to expect from the future, but I think we will still be poor! Our sons go to school; there is one nearby and it is free of cost. We have to buy the necessary books, but if you show the bill at school they give you the money back. It would be nice if our sons could get a paid job when they leave school, but I'm not sure that there will be any work available for them. At night, before the children go to bed, I sometimes sing to them or tell them stories about the lives of kings and queens and people who, unlike us, are very, very rich!

Khedani Devi Tells the Story of the Poor Brahmin

The Story of the Poor Priest's Cow

Once upon a time there lived a Brahmin priest and his wife. They were very poor and tried to make ends meet through begging. One day the priest reached the king's palace. The king was a good man and used to help the poor. The king offered the priest some rice and a cow. The priest and his wife were very happy with the gifts. Soon they became rich by selling the cow's milk.

One day while the Brahmin's wife was cleaning her courtyard, she found the cow staring at her. The cow did not stop staring and she became so afraid of the cow that she wanted to get rid of it. At night when her husband came home, she told him about how the cow had been staring at her and asked him to take the cow back to the king. At first her husband did not want to lose the cow which had made them so rich. But when he saw how afraid his wife was, he finally agreed.

The cow begged the Brahmin not to send her back to the king but leave her somewhere in the forest. The priest agreed. In the forest the cow met a tigress and the cow begged the tigress not to kill her. The tigress said, 'I will not eat you because in this dense jungle I am alone, now you are here, we can become good friends.' They started living together. During the day both of them used to go in search of their food and at night they made their home near a well.

And so as time passed they slept by the well and then both gave birth, to a calf and cub respectively. The cub and the calf considered themselves as brothers and were inseparable.

One day the cow went to the nearby river to drink water. While drinking, some saliva from her mouth dropped into the water. At the same time the tigress was drinking downstream. She swallowed the saliva from the cow. The tigress found the saliva so delicious that she thought: 'If the saliva was so delicious, how delicious would the flesh itself be, so maybe I'll eat the cow.' In the evening when both the cow and tigress returned home, the tigress realised how delicious the cow's smell was and she decided to eat the cow. When she told the cow her plan, the cow replied: 'Well friend, if you really want to eat me, I cannot stop you.'

The cow went to her calf and said, 'Your aunt the tigress wants to eat me, so one day I may not come home.'

The next day, as usual, the cow and the tigress went in search of food. At night the tigress came home alone and when the calf asked where his mother was the tigress lied: 'Well, she is not coming to live with us any more.' The calf told the cub about what the cow had said the night before. Hearing this, the cub decided to teach his mother a lesson and asked her to bring some grass from near the well for the calf. When the tigress was collecting the grass, the cub pushed her into the well and she drowned.

After this the cub decided to protect the calf. He helped him when in trouble and they lived for a long time happily together.

— *Marieke van Vliet*

A Long Way from Home

Tamang family in Sikharbesi working on the land

5

Maya Lama

A Long Way from Home

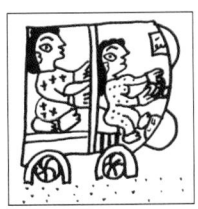 SIKHARBESI IS SITUATED in the district of Nuwakot, a mountainous area north of Kathmandu. Inhabited by Tamang, Damai, Chhettri and Brahmin groups the area is quite poor and only partly accessible by road. There is no electricity, and many people are illiterate. The main occupation of most local people is agriculture, but the maize and millet cultivated on the steep slopes is often not enough to feed the family for the whole year and many have turned to prostitution as an alternative means of earning money. Many families in Nuwakot district, and also the districts of Sindhupalchowk, Khavre and Dhading, are involved in the trade of young girls. In some villages inhabited only by Tamangs, up to ninety per cent of the families are involved in this trade.

Prostitution and the trade in girls are not new phenomena in Nepal. Two forms of traditional prostitution have long existed, *deuki*, the practice of offering young girls to a temple and *badini*, which is prostitution by the untouchable *Badi* caste. Both forms are illegal but are gradually changing into modern forms of urban prostitution. Between 1850 and 1951, Nepal was ruled by the Rana families who used to send their servants to recruit young girls from villages, usually those situated north of Kathmandu, to work in their palaces. There they served as maids or concubines and some even became 'queens'. After the end of Rana rule, flesh traffickers found a large market in India and it is estimated that at least 200,000 Nepali girls are working as prostitutes in Indian brothels.

Girls from the hills, especially Tamang girls, are very popular in India because of their light skin and Mongolian features. In some cases parents sell their daughters, or husbands sell their wives, but many girls are tricked away from their families and sold by brokers for a price of around 25,000 rupees. The girls then have to work for at least five years to 'repay' this debt. Some of the girls, attracted by the clothes, jewellery and money of those who return from India, decide to go themselves, not realising what will happen to them. Some husbands send their wives to the brothels and then live off their earnings. Most of the women are illiterate and those who return remain silent about how they earned their money, because talking openly about their experiences may lead to social isolation and they want to rebuild their life in the community.

Nowadays, two non-governmental organisations are active in Sikharbesi. One of them, the Women's Rehabilitation Centre (WOREC), works in the field of community development, mobilising women who have been socially rejected and who face discrimination. Women from the community are trained to implement programmes in their own society so some of the girls give extension messages about AIDS. Maya Lama is one of the most active village women and, as both a teacher and leader of a women's group, she makes a contribution towards a better condition of life in Sikharbesi.

Maya Lama

Maya Lama is an attractive woman who lives in one of the Tamang villages in the Sikharbesi area. We had heard that she once worked as a prostitute in Bombay and that she was the only one in Sikharbesi who did not mind talking about it. We meet her as she is coming back from the field and she walks ahead of us up the hill to her house. After inviting us into the kitchen she takes out a 'safe home delivery kit' provided by an NGO and shows us how she demonstrates the use of the kit to the village women. 'Look', she says while squatting on the floor, 'the baby will fall onto the plastic sheet. One woman used the kit and we cut the umbilical cord with the razor blade provided. Personally, I found the experience quite disgusting and it made me feel sick; for two days I couldn't eat a thing!'

Maya tells her story in a lively and spontaneous way with the occasional sentence in English but she remains, at the same time, very careful about what she says. She denies ever working as a prostitute in Bombay, but she quite openly describes what she saw in the brothel where she was taken against her will. She shows us an album containing photos of herself and her family. All the pictures of her are taken in modern houses and she is wearing either an expensive sari or very modern clothes and is either sitting or lying on a bed. Some photos have been torn in half.

Maya Lama

Maya Lama Tells Her Life Story

The Promise

My name is Maya Lama. I am twenty-seven years old and come from a big family of two brothers and seven sisters. There were two more sisters as well but they died. Our family was poor and often there was not enough food and hardly any money for clothes so we wore only simple ones. I did not go to school, as there was no school in this village when I was young.

When I was about fifteen years old one of the women in our village promised me a job in Kathmandu. I knew that my parents would never let me go so I decided not to tell them about it. I wanted to earn money and buy beautiful clothes and jewellery like some other women in our village. I left my house in the middle of the night without telling anybody, walked to the road in the pitch dark and, together with the woman took a bus. I trusted her because she was a woman but when it became light I looked out of the window and found that we were travelling to India instead of Kathmandu.

We arrived in Bombay and went to a big house. I was taken to a room in which there were at least fifty other girls, some of them only twelve years old. I started to worry, and after looking around, I began to suspect something was wrong. I couldn't work out what we were doing there. I questioned some of the girls who replied that they made sweaters and could earn up to 3,000 rupees a month. Then, after a while I was taken to another room with nice furniture. Somebody put red lipstick on my lips, but I did not want to wear it, so I wiped it off; a little later I had to put it on again. I became scared. A man came in and then went off to the room with the girls along with an older woman. When they were not looking I ran outside but someone else saw me and four people pursued and caught me.

They brought me back and locked me up in a room; I was beaten all over my body, even on my face, they did not give me any food or drink so I was forced to drink water from the toilet. Fifteen days later they took me back to the brothel and there I saw what was really going on: when a client came we had to line up in a row and the client would choose one of us who had to go upstairs to have sex. We were watched over by a madam, who was called the 'manager'. When she wasn't looking I tried to hide behind others in the row. A brothel consists of several rooms, each with its own manager. About twenty girls are put in one room and each girl has to serve between ten and fifteen clients per day. In the morning the girls are given a meal but in the evening they must pay for a meal with money that is earned through asking for tips from clients. The client pays the money for their services directly to the manager. Six months later I tried to escape again and this time they did not catch me. This period was altogether the most traumatic, sad and difficult one of my entire life; in my own village I have never been that unhappy.

Seeking Solace in Tamang Songs

Having escaped, I walked the streets, as I had no place to stay. By chance I met some people who were willing to help me. One of them was a Nepali man who had lived near my village and who said I could stay with them. They worked in a school and the man whom I had met before taught me to read and write. I started to sell things in order to survive and later one of them bought me a plane ticket to Mysore where they said I could earn more money through business. During this time I often felt lonely and homesick; I had no friends so to comfort myself I bought a notebook in which I wrote down the songs from my village which we had sung while working in the fields when I was young.

> *Living with parents, without knowing,*
> *One passes one's youth, I think,*
> *Long ago the dove was gold,*
> *But because of ill-fate I have suffered in this life.*
> *Oh! Lama's drum, Jhankri's drum,*
> *I have suffered in an alien place,*
> *I wished I could die without pain and go to heaven.*

Back Home Again

When I was nineteen years old, I decided to go back home; I had saved about 9,000 rupees which was plenty and I missed my family. It took me two days by train to Gorakhpur on the Indian border, then a bus ride, and for the last part to the village, I had to walk. My parents were so happy to see me again; they cried because they felt both happy and sad at the same time when they saw me again at last.

I got married in the same year that I returned. I remember it as a wonderful day — we sang a lot and I wore beautiful clothes. Now I live together with my husband in this house. My parents live just above here on the top of the hill. We would like to have children but I have had two miscarriages and now I am scared. I have become thin so I want to start taking birth control pills. I don't think it is a good idea for me to try to get pregnant again as it seems that I cannot have any children.

These days my time is spent working in our fields and we have a small shop in which we sell cigarettes, biscuits, batteries, sweets and soap. Sometimes we go to the village of Samundratar, about two hours walk from here, where they show Hindi and Hong Kong films on video. I enjoy seeing these films very much, and Bruce Lee is one of my favourite actors! I also have some movie magazines brought from Kathmandu; it's fun to read about the movie stars and see their pictures.

Maya and the children of her class near her house in Sikharbesi

Classes in the Courtyard

When I heard about a training programme that was being given locally by the Save the Children organisation I went there to find out more. They formed women's groups in the area and I was chosen as a leader. During the training I learnt new skills such as the use of a delivery kit and information about AIDS and I now pass on this information to other women. Sometimes, I also assist the WOREC office with organising meetings or translating from the Tamang language into Nepali.

For the last two years I have been working for the WOREC office as a teacher as well. I heard that they were looking for a local teacher but had thought that nobody here was literate so I went to their office to tell them I was interested. I think it is important to educate people; not many people in this village have had a chance to learn. I teach twenty children from this village, with ages varying from five to fourteen years, in the morning from seven to ten o'clock, and in the evening I teach adults. I get great pleasure from this work.

Children of Maya's class

While climbing up to Maya's house we can hear the children in her class singing a song: 'We do not have to buy the book, the book is free!' The children, dressed mostly in old clothes, sit in a circle in Maya's courtyard, their books on the ground before them. Maya asks them what they

66

learnt today and the children repeat the letters in chorus. 'Time to go', Maya says; the children grab their books, say 'Namaste' and then rush down the steep hill, yelling and stumbling. 'Look out, be careful!' shouts Maya.

'And now I need a cigarette!' she says. Her quick eyes notice a girl on the top of the hill busy sowing maize in the fields. 'Hey! I missed you today, where were you?' she shouts to the girl. 'Make sure you come tomorrow!'

Talking about AIDS and Bombay

In my opinion the situation in our village has improved. Before there was no school, but now there is one and there are also classes for adults. There is now a health post and vaccinations are available. Information about AIDS is also given; it was only three years ago that I heard about it for the first time myself but now many people here are aware about AIDS. I, myself, tell people about what I have seen in Bombay. Women who return from Bombay do not talk about what is happening there: they usually lie and say that it was good there and that you can earn lots of money. I tell the truth: I warn girls not to believe the stories they hear about good jobs. I warn them not to go to Bombay.

— *Eva Kipp and Marieke van Vliet*

'You have to go through sad times to know the good times'

Sparsely forested hills near Saahilakomda

(Photo by Marieke van Vliet)

6

Bakuli Khawar

'You have to go through sad times to know the good times'

SAAHILAKOMDA IS A small village of fifty-one households in the district of Salyan in the mid-western region of Nepal. It is situated in the hills about one hour's walk away from the district headquarters, also called Salyan, where there are shops with electricity and a bus stop. The people in Saahilakomda are mainly farmers, although the area is very dry and production is dependent on rainfall. Nevertheless, all families are able to grow enough to feed themselves and are sometimes able to produce enough surplus to sell. Some men migrate to India to earn additional income, returning just before the rainy season to help the family in the busiest season with agricultural work.

The village is attractive and peaceful. Houses are constructed of stone with a mud matrix and have wooden windows and doors, some of which show intricate woodcarvings. In the more remote parts of the district there are vast areas of forest, but in Saahilakomda and around the district headquarters, deforestation is a serious problem.

Bakuli Khawar

Bakuli is a firm, cheerful, good-humoured woman who has a very positive approach to the things in life. She talks with great enthusiasm and deep concern about her work in the local Forest Users' Group but also recounts some of the more painful experiences in her life. She is dressed in clothes, which are neat rather than expensive. When we arrive at her house, she takes us inside to show us photographs of her husband when he was in the army and some family pictures on the wall. She complains that her radio is broken. Her grandson slipped and dropped the radio on the ground and now it is not working anymore.

Bakuli Khawar
(*Photo by Alieke Barmentloo*)

Bakuli Khawar Tells Her Life Story

My Family and Marriage

You ask me how old I am but I'm not really sure since nobody ever told me when I was born. I think I must be about fifty-five years old. I am the eldest in our family and have two brothers and quite a few sisters. One brother left for India and we never saw him again; the other brother and a sister live here in Saahilakomda and two other sisters live in nearby villages. We often visit each other and enjoy a good chat. Although very old now, our mother is still alive and lives nearby.

I have nice memories of my wedding. I was quite young, only about fourteen years old, and I only knew what was going to happen four or five days beforehand. When they told me I felt quite sad — I didn't know what to do, where they would take me and how they would treat me. My parents made a special place for worship and performed the ritual of *kanyaadaan*, which is done just before giving away a daughter in marriage. The procession with the bridegroom arrived the evening before the marriage ceremony. They stayed the whole day and feasted with us. All the rituals surrounding the marriage were performed at my parents' house and I enjoyed that very much. Then in the evening I was carried to my new home by my parents.

My husband's home is quite near our house, so I knew him before we were married and he seemed to be a good man. When we reached his home a special ceremony was performed at the entrance to welcome me into the house as the new bride and relatives were provided with food. At the time I had mixed feelings, both happy and unhappy, but it is necessary for women to marry and leave their own house and family.

Wedding Gifts

For my wedding gifts or dowry, my parents gave me cooking pots, a water pot, dishes, bowls, clothes, a quilt, a mattress and a cow. During the *kanyaadaan* ceremony one needs to catch hold of a cow's tail; that cow is then given as a gift. In those days it was traditional to give useful household goods, but now that has changed and if you want to get your daughter married you have to spend a lot of money. A dowry can be made up of all kinds of fancy goods nowadays including a watch or a television and really wealthy people in other parts of the country even give a car, bus or house.

In our community the parents of the boy have to bring gifts of sweets, and a goat which is killed for a feast. The parents of the girl give beds, mattresses, clothes and kitchen utensils. Both sets of parents and relatives give a 'good luck' *tika* and some money known as *dakshina*. We cannot afford such expensive gifts, we just sing and dance to celebrate the marriage. One dance from the district of Dang, to the south of here, is particularly popular in this area. The older men in the community carry big drums and sing while performing a special dance known as *Sorathi*. The women carry smaller drums and sing all night long. I like to dance and to sing both religious and love songs but we elderly people don't know how to dance to all these modern songs we have no idea what to do with our feet!

A Lonely Time

My in-laws were good people, but even so, I found the first few years of married life a bit difficult. In my parents' home I had been freer and I had to get used to my new life. I was also alone, because my husband was in the Nepalese army. Then my husband's parents died within a short span of time while our eldest children were still very young. I felt very sad at this loss and missed them a lot.

After twenty years in the army my husband retired and receives a pension of only five hundred rupees a month. Who can live on that? He had no option but to take up another job and became the guard of the bank in the village of Thamare, which is about a five-hour walk towards Rukum district. It is not a good place. My husband is a good man — well, he was a good man. Thamare is even colder than Saahilakomda in the winter. You know how it is, it is cold and you have to stay on duty all night and so you need something warm and when the tea shops are all closed, you turn to alcohol. It warms you and makes you feel less lonely. But alcohol is not your friend; it is an enemy. It tells you 'I am your friend, stay with me,' but if you stay with it long enough, it deserts you and leaves you alone with all your problems.

Finally, my husband's drinking problem affected his stomach. He started to get terrible pains and went to a doctor who gave him expensive medicines and told him not to drink anymore. For a while he stopped, but when he went back to Thamare the trouble started all over again. It is not only the cold and the loneliness; the people there are just no good. It is a trading place with lots of strangers who drink a lot. Now five years later, my husband has retired from this job as well and stays at home. Sometimes he still has bouts of drinking; if I talk about it, I feel like crying, but that does not help. I am not only worried about the waste of money — since he started drinking so much he has not been the same anymore. All his energy has gone and he just sits doing nothing, and that is not good.

My husband had already joined the Nepalese army before we got married. There were also two other men from this village in the army. I found it very difficult when I was alone and our children were young. I had to do all the work myself and look after the children. Although he would send us money and clothes, my husband's visits home were irregular — sometimes once a year, sometimes more and sometimes less. Even on the major festivals he was not always present, as he couldn't always take leave. I had to work in the fields alone and if my husband was home he would come and help with the ploughing, but he was not home often; I usually had to work for other people who in turn would help me with the ploughing.

When the children grew up life became a bit easier, as they could do so much to help and, finally, I had some company. You have to go through sad times to know the good times. Altogether we had six children, two sons and four daughters, but we lost one daughter. Our eldest daughter went to India with her husband after she married. I've heard that they now have two children but I've never seen them. I think they must be too busy to visit us, which I find rather sad. Our eldest son lives with his wife and their son in this house. He is still studying and is

Bakuli in front of her house
(Photo by Alieke Barmentloo)

looking for a job while he waits for the results of his exams. My second daughter is also married; she lives nearby and I see her quite often.

The other two children still go to school. I sent all the children to school because it is important to be able to read and write, not only to find a job, but also for yourself. When I was young there was no school and I didn't have the opportunity to go to school, but I would have loved to. Sometimes I feel so silly that I cannot read or write and I do not want my children to have that feeling. Some months ago my husband bought a radio, and I was really pleased. Although I can't read, I can listen to the news and to the programmes of Nepali folk songs. Sometimes I enjoy listening to dramas and to the Agricultural Development and Forestry Programmes — they provide one with such useful information, but since my grandson slipped and fell yesterday the radio doesn't work anymore.

Chairwoman of the Forest Users' Group

I am currently the chairwoman of our local Forest Users' Group. Some years ago, with the help of the government Women's Development Office a group was formed to start reforestation. We village women had to work in the forest planting trees for which we were paid, and we then used that money to build a school. We did all the work ourselves and only had to buy cement and materials for the roof. My sister was the chairwoman of the group, but as she had young children, it was too difficult for her so they chose me instead. My children are not that young anymore and I am not scared to speak out. I think it is of the utmost importance for women to raise their voices when it is in their own interest — the forest is important both for our children and us.

There are no *saal* trees in our forest but we need the broad, flat leaves of this particular tree to make plates called *tapari* for our festivals. We had the right to take the leaves from another forest owned by a nearby village but they won't give us the leaves anymore, and sometimes we have to fight for them. Now we will have our own *saal* trees because we sowed them ourselves. I enjoy the work; it is important, not only because we need these trees but also because I am worried about the future of my children. There isn't much forest left and if we don't do anything the last trees will disappear and our children will suffer. We have to plant new trees and protect the forest. In the past, we women were ignorant and cut the trees until we saw that our own forest was slowly disappearing.

The work takes up a lot of my time. I have to visit other houses to meet all my 'sisters and brothers' in the village so I can motivate and organise them, then I must also visit public offices. Some people say that I only do it for the money but I don't actually get any money. If I go to an office for this work I sit on a chair and sometimes get a cup of tea and a snack, nothing more. I don't have enough time, which is why the work is so difficult for me. The work itself is not a problem but when I come home there are my own chores to do as well. In fact, I was so busy with the forestry business that I was late planting the rice and keeping up with the housework. That is why I find it so difficult — if it weren't so important I would have given it up long ago.

Through my association with this forestry group I have been on a study tour through Nepal. We visited Pokhara, Palpa and Lumbini to see the forests there and to find out how they were managed. It was a wonderful experience to visit those places, especially Pokhara, which is so developed. Many people have also been here to visit us. Even foreigners come to observe the work of our Forest Users' Group; they look at and see the forest, and talk with us. At one time, the Forest Officer promised me a study tour abroad because, as chairwoman, I had done such a lot of good work, but then America did not send enough money and there were funds only for one person, so they chose a man. I am so disappointed; I would have loved to go to these far away places like Thailand and the Philippines but I don't think I will ever get that chance again. It is a bad habit — they come and look and make you happy with their promises and then they cancel it all.

Problems with Water

In our village we have a serious water shortage — there is just not enough to go round. About ten years ago a storage tank and three taps were constructed to bring water from a village up above our own. However, because of a dispute over the right to use the water, the people of the other village cut our pipeline six months after the system had been completed. We were trying to solve the water problem by visiting various offices, but then the elections came so we discussed the situation with the leaders of the different parties and promised to vote for the party who would give us water, finally making a deal with the Congress Party. I have now heard that every ward will get 300,000 rupees from the government, so there should now be enough money, and the leaders have assured us that they will provide us with water.

In total we have three *ropani* (1 *ropani* = 608.4 sq yds) of irrigated fields and seven *ropani* of unirrigated land. Normally, this is enough to feed us, and if there is a good harvest, we can sell a little surplus. But it all depends on the rainfall, if there is enough rain we are able to sell grain and if not we have only enough for ourselves. We have some fruit trees as well — orange, lychee, papaya, mango and apple, and my husband sells the fruits.

Religion

We are from the *Jogi* caste. We worship the gods Mahadev and Vishnu, and every night when we go to bed or if we have a problem, we chant 'Jaya Bhagawan'. There is also a temple of the goddess Bhagawati in the village of Khairabang but it takes us four hours to get there, so now we women want our own temple in this village. At present we only have a temple consisting of wooden poles and every year around May or June we perform a special ceremony of worship for rain in which we put a new pole in the temple.

Behind the temple there is a graveyard where all our ancestors are buried. In the *Jogi* caste it is traditional to bury our dead rather than the usual Hindu practice of burning them, but we celebrate all other festivals in the same way as other Hindus. *Dashain* is fun, as there are so many people about and we can eat lots of good food, but I think *Tihar* and the women's festival *Teej* are the most pleasant ones. *Teej* is the best festival because of all the singing and dancing, but during *Tihar* all my sisters come here to give our brothers a special *tika* signifying good luck for the year and this is a good chance to see all the family again.

— *Alieke Barmentloo and Marieke van Vliet*

Political Visions
and New Gods

7

Laxmi Baskota

Political Visions and New Gods

DEMOCRACY IS A relatively new phenomenon in Nepal, where for centuries the political scene was marked by the reign of one absolute ruler after the other. In April 1990, following a massive popular uprising, the partyless 'Panchayat' system was replaced with democracy. Four years later the Unified Marxists and Leninists (UML) were elected to office and have formed a so-called Communist government.

Women in Nepal have been recorded to participate in politics since the last century. Women joined uprisings against the Rana regime and the partyless 'Panchayat' system. However, in general, women's involvement in politics has been limited. Relatively few women have reached a position of power in the country, and currently not a single female minister can be found in the cabinet. Only a few women are active as politicians at the district and local level.

In 1991 when June Maya Praja went to vote for the first time she did not have much of a choice. 'The men of the village said there were boxes with different drawings on them, like a sun and a tree,' June Maya remembers. 'We were told to put our mark next to the sign of a tree.' Although this is still the reality in some villages, the attitude of rural women in general towards politics is changing. Women who attend literacy classes become more aware of the effect of politics in their daily life. Young women who have had the chance to go to school have greater awareness about politics and some, like Laxmi Baskota, decide to get involved with political activities.

Laxmi Baskota

When women are politically active
people spread rumours about them.

One active Communist woman who joined demonstrations and put up posters during the 1994 elections is a student from Baglung Bazar named Laxmi Baskota. When we meet her it has just been announced that the Unified Marxists and Leninists (UML) have won both the local and national elections. Her hometown, the headquarters of a rugged district in the western region of Nepal, is covered with reminders of the recent election. Symbols of the various parties decorate every pole, building, stone, and temple, while active locals use the walls of their houses to display their political convictions. In Baglung, caste differences are rigid; most of the people are subsistence farmers, but they are often unable to provide their families with sufficient food. In this area, the victory of UML has instilled a feeling of hope and expectation in the local people.

We meet Laxmi in the sitting room of the family house. It is of traditional design with tiny hallways connecting the many rooms, including a chicken run on the first floor and a kitchen made out of aluminium sheeting attached to the back. Laxmi, aged twenty-one, looks like a

Laxmi Baskota

schoolgirl dressed in her simple outfit of a blue skirt and woollen sweater. Unlike most Nepali women she wears no ornaments and even refuses to allow her grandmother to apply a *tika* to her forehead, since, as she says, 'Mao has become my god.' In the living room Laxmi has replaced the pictures of Hindu gods with those of Mao Tse Tung and has developed her own vision for a just Nepali society. In Laxmi's ideal Nepal there is no caste system, poverty is non-existent and nobody tells women what to do and what not to do. She does realise, however, that there are many obstacles in the way, one of them being her grandmother.

Laxmi Baskota

Woman with a Mission

Many people like to make a lot of money in life, but I am not that kind of person. During my trips to poor villages I have seen the problems of women and their families. I feel sorry for them. That's why in my life I want to help to improve the condition of poor people.

I am a member of a Nepali Communist Party called Mashal; my mother inspired me to become an active member after the death of my father. She is from a village in which most people support the Communists and she used to tell me about Communism when I was a child. However, up to my father's death a few years ago no one in my family spoke openly about this. He was a policeman and was not in favour of Communism. Also, before democracy, people could not openly support democratic parties. If they did, they were seen as enemies of the country and suppressed.

A New 'Religion'

After democracy I stopped going to temples, performing Hindu *puja* and wearing a *tika*, and put up posters of Mao in the living room. I adore Mao in the same way as my grandmother adores the goddess Laxmi. I respect him because he has established Communism in China. Laxmi does not talk to us and she has not given us any principles. Similarly, Mao cannot talk to us, but at least he has given us some practical guidelines — that is why Mao is my god. I don't worship him, I just adore him and his principles, that's all.

I am inspired by his writings but I find it hard to apply his principles in daily life. In order to apply new ideas we first need to change our thinking. But the problem is, we cannot change ourselves because of our society. We are influenced by our society and we cannot just forget about that. We cannot change our life as told in a book. Still, we have to work in the society. If we could only turn all these wonderful ideas into reality, then our lives would be so much better.

Laxmi in her room. On the wall, a calendar with pictures of important Communist leaders

Women and Politics

Many of our Nepali people think that Communism is not good, so they dislike it. They believe it is better to work hard and to do good business instead of joining a political party. They think that being young, we should make money by working in an office or something similar. Most people don't like to see young women working for a party. They believe politics is not for women and when women do take an active part in politics, people spread rumours about them. We suffer in this way. In Nepal very few women are active in politics. In Baglung there are just ten of us. Many support the party, but they cannot be active because of problems at home. Their families do not allow them to go to the field. That's the problem with women and politics.

I am working for a women's group which is part of the party, called the All Nepal Women's Association. Our organisation has started some programmes to stop alcohol abuse and gambling. We go from village to village and meet poor women. The fact is men dominate them and we inspire village women to fight for their rights, to become educated, like men. I meet many poor low caste women; they live a very miserable life. Most of them don't have enough food to feed their families, and eat only one meal a day, either in the morning or in the evening. They cannot even send their children to school. Village women know nothing about politics, and they just vote for the same party as their fathers and husbands. Whoever the men tell them to vote for, they have to vote for. When going to the village we never tell them we are Communists but the people know, since no other party member will visit poor people when it's not election time.

Visiting Villages

In one month, I spend about ten days in the field. I sometimes travel with my friends, but when they are not around I travel alone. Sometimes the boys in the villages trouble me by calling me names or following me, but I am not afraid, and try to talk sense to them. My family understands me and does not prevent me from going to the field — only my grandmother cannot understand why I would want to do this, and always warns me when I go out.

In Nepal we have not found equality yet, even though the Communist principle says that poor and rich, men and women are equal. It's quite impossible to have equality in our society, since the party is just starting. Also, the party can't do anything unless people are aware and educated. They must be willing to follow the rules of the Communist Party. It is people who have drawn a line between rich and poor. Influential people have invented a caste system, so that they can dominate other people in the name of religion. I hope the caste system will disappear soon. All these divisions are made by people and should be abolished by people. In my family people from all castes are allowed to enter the house. And yes, we treat everyone the same as Brahmins. There's only one little problem, my grandmother is still prejudiced and she dislikes it when low caste people come to visit us.

As far as marriage is concerned, I think I am still too young for that. I believe we should not get married at an early age. My eldest sister had a 'run-away' marriage, though I am free to choose my own husband. I would like to marry someone who is a member of the Communist Party; he should be honest and educated as well. If I pass the Intermediate exams in Law I will try to go to Pokhara for further studies. After that I will continue to serve the Communist Party and work for the betterment of the poor people.

A Traveller's Tale from Laxmi Baskota

Once I went to a village called Okhale. I was on my own and at eight o'clock in the evening I reached a small, lonely house in the forest. Since the bazaar was far away from that place, I realised I would have to stay there. There was a woman with one son studying in class ten in school and some daughters. I asked the woman if she would allow me to spend the night at her place. At first she refused because she was frightened. Whenever that family met new people they became scared, as they were completely separated from society.

After some time she invited me in and gave me some food. After the meal, one of the daughters became friendly with me. I asked her about her studies and she started to cry. She said: 'My brother goes to school, but my mother doesn't allow me to go. I want to learn how to read and write like my brother.' She then asked me to talk to her mother. I did so, but the mother said she could not afford the school fees. What's more, she needed the girl to look after her son and younger daughters. She thought it was not necessary to educate girls.

— Lucia de Vries

Life in the High Pastures

Sherpa family in a shelter or *goth* near Yale

8

Lamseki Sherpa
Life in the High Pastures

 ALL OVER NEPAL animal husbandry is practised in a variety of different forms according to the local natural environment and the cultural heritage of the various groups following this way of life. During the monsoon many herders move with their livestock and families to the high pastures at an altitude of up to 5,000 metres where they live in temporary shelters or *goths* made from woven bamboo mats, stones and branches. These open meadowlands lie above the tree line and are often shrouded in clouds or swirling mists which may clear to reveal the surrounding snow-capped peaks. Women who have been brought up in the high pastures or who have spent much of their life there are usually highly independent and often run the *goths* on their own while their menfolk look after the house and crops down in the permanent village settlements.

Tamang, Magar and Gurung herders usually rear goats and sheep, for meat and wool respectively, whereas the Sherpas who have settled in the highlands above 2,200 metres rear pure yaks in the higher pastures and crossbred varieties of yak and common cattle in the lower areas. These crossbreeds of yak and cow, known as *dzum* and *dimzo*, are raised for their milk. The herders consume some milk while the remainder is converted into butter and a dry type of cheese, both of which can be bartered for grains or sold for cash at local markets. Nowadays, many herders sell their fresh milk directly to a cheese factory if there is one in the vicinity.

Returns from raising livestock in this way have never been particularly high, but nowadays herders are confronted with more complex problems. It is becoming increasingly difficult to feed the animals because there is less grassland and forest area left for grazing. Furthermore, fewer family members are available to carry food from the permanent village settlements up to

89

the high pastures, so the herders have to hire porters to do this for them which costs extra money. A third problem is the education of children — the *goths* are far away from the village so it is impossible to continue school while in the high pastures. These problems have resulted in some herders deciding to sell their livestock and giving up their original way of life.

Lamseki Sherpa

Lamseki was born thirty-five years ago in the little village of Tsanku in the mountains south of Rolwaling. The village is inhabited mainly by Sherpa and Gurung people who are almost all livestock herders. Lamseki has spent virtually all her life up in the high pastures herding her parents' five goats and sixteen yak hybrids, often going up to 5,000 metres with the yaks. Because her parents had no sons and she was the eldest daughter, Lamseki continued to herd the animals owned by her parents even after she was married. She now has three sons and two small daughters of her own ranging in age between six months and thirteen years.

The family has now given up their *goths* in the high pastures and has settled permanently in Tsanku village. The day we visited Lamseki at home she was back from the fields quite late just as darkness fell. She had been harvesting millet and remarked with a grin that it had been a heavy day, as she is not used to this kind of work. Nevertheless, she immediately got on with preparing the evening meal.

The whole family lives with Lamseki's mother on the first and second floor of the farm while Lamseki's younger sister and her four children live on the ground floor. Lamseki decided that she should take a rest for a few days but the next day she is still preparing food and drinks for the many guests who drop in, only taking a short break now and then to smoke a cigarette or feed the baby. She doesn't even attend the three days of ceremonies in the village temple that are being performed for the father of the village Lama who died last year.

Lamseki rules the household in a resolute manner giving her husband some money out of her purse when he asks for it. The two of them discuss the suitability of a new school for the eldest son who is about to finish the fifth grade. In between tea and the drinks of local alcohol that she frequently serves, we talk with Lamseki about her life. She loved being with the animals up in the high pastures and gives us long, detailed descriptions of her experiences. After some hesitation she also sings a little song about marriage.

Lamseki Sherpa

Lamseki with her family in front of their house in Tsanku

Lamseki Sherpa Tells Her Life Story

Early Life

When I was young the forest was the only thing I knew about; I was not aware that there was any existence other than the one we followed in the high pastures. I didn't even know the difference between a house and a *goth*. When I saw a house for the first time I was really surprised as it was made entirely of stone. I remember thinking 'Oh-ho, what a tall roof for a *goth*; it reaches right up to the sky.' When I saw people thrashing millet for the first time I was puzzled and couldn't understand why people were so busy beating the ground.

I have two sisters, two and six years younger. As children we played with dolls that we made ourselves from things we found lying around outside, and we also played with branches of trees. Sometimes I would quarrel with my sisters: if one of them insisted that something belonged to her and we others disagreed we would have a fight. I always won because I was the biggest, but my parents always took sides with my little sister and called us names. My parents also got angry with us when we broke or mislaid things and they beat us with their hands or with a stick. When I was angry I just stared straight ahead and pretended not to hear anything. If I had done something really awful I would keep silent — at those times I would be very frightened.

From about my sixth to my thirteenth year I did what my parents told me to do, whether it was collecting firewood, fetching water or taking the animals to graze and bringing them back to the *goth*. I started to milk the yak hybrids when I was nine years old but in those days the milk was not sold and we used to make yoghurt, butter and *churpi*, a hard dry cheese. The milk was converted into butter by transforming it first into yoghurt. When I was a little older we started to make cheese by pressing it between two stones.

In about twenty days we could fill a large *doko* with cheese and exchange it for an equal volume of grains, but nowadays, grains are much more expensive and not easily available. The clarified butter was sold in Kathmandu. In the early days the motorable road which now runs from Dolakha through Charikot to Kathmandu had not been built and all produce had to be carried to the market.

When I was about thirteen years old my parents settled permanently in the village of Tsanku and from then on I had to take care of the *goth* with my sisters. It was a bit difficult but we managed to do all the necessary work and my father would come up from the village every six days to bring food for us, and to see how we were getting on. We never had a shortage of food unlike many of the other people who had to borrow from neighbours. The food we ate up there was not so different from what we would eat when we were at home. I think we ate a few more wild mushrooms, young bamboo shoots and *magan*, a green leafy vegetable and a lot of *tsampa*, a flour made from roasted barley. Down in the village we ate more wild ferns and nettles from the forest. Rice, millet, maize and wheat were our staple foods both in the *goth* and at home.

The *goth* in which we lived up in the high pastures was temporary and I could both make and move it myself. Before leaving at the end of the season we would hide the poles and beams behind the bushes for the next year and we would carry only the bamboo mats and the kitchen utensils on to the next place. In the months between May and September we would move to the highest pastures where there were no trees so we had to take the poles with us as well. We had *dimzo* hybrids in our herd and a hardy type of goat so we would take them to the cooler pastures high above where the last *Dhupi* pine tree grows. It would take us a whole month to get up to the highest place, from the moment we started to move.

Up at that height it is very cold and there are frequent hailstorms. Once it starts to snow we would come down. Even if it is raining, or just cloudy and cold, you cannot stay inside the *goth* but must go out to watch the animals, especially the hybrids. I think this is the hardest part of life up there as well as climbing tall trees in the lower forests to cut fodder. The best part of living in the *goth* is that there are always plenty of milk products to eat and drink.

If it rained, we would cover ourselves with *ghum*, a homemade shield of bamboo and leaves. It was only about fifteen years ago that umbrellas and plastic sheets became available. When it snowed we would wear thick clothes and try to shake the snow off because if it melts on your clothes you get very cold. In the high mountains we had to have shoes and socks and some of us wore boots. We used to put our wet shoes near the fire and the next morning they would always be dry. If we went above the last of the pine trees we would not get bitten by leeches, but below there are always a lot of them in the grass during the monsoon. The children always cry and make a great fuss when they find a leech but adults just pull the leech off and throw it away.

Marriage

I was eighteen years old when a lama from Dungje came to ask my parents if I could marry his son; the lama had seen me in the village when he came here to perform a religious ceremony.

My parents did not like the idea. I had not even thought about getting married at that stage but only wished that my future husband should stay with me and should be friendly, kind and honest. Later, I met Tendi, the lama's son, in the *goth* and we fell in love. Two years after we had met, Tendi and his father came again to ask for me and this time the marriage was arranged.

Quite soon after my marriage, my sisters' marriages were also arranged. They started to live with their husbands as is the usual case but I took over the running of my parents' *goth* because I was the eldest daughter. My parents had three daughters so they divided their property into three parts and gave us one part each. My husband's property is in Dungje but we live on the property that I got from my parents. I did not go to Dungje to live with him there but stayed with my parents. Along with the livestock I also took over a loan that my parents had taken. We found it impossible to pay back the loan by just selling milk, so I sold some of the yak hybrids too. Later, I was able to buy part of the land belonging to my sisters as well.

Last year a government survey team came to measure and register all land in the village, and our land was registered in my husband's name. Any money that we have earned has been through the efforts of both of us, so it doesn't really matter in whose name the land is registered as it is eventually for our children anyway. Both of us have a say in how our money is spent, and neither of us would ever spend money without informing the other. We even discuss what we will spend on food and clothes and what we can save. I am always happy when Tendi brings me what he has earned outside the village, too.

Four of my children were born in the *goth*, some of them really high up in the mountains where there are no trees. I was not afraid to deliver up there, as like in the village, there are neighbours who will help you. There are many other women in the world who also have to deliver in such conditions. It was no problem for me as I was used to staying there alone. When my husband went down to fetch food three times a month I always stayed behind, and because the children were with me I did not feel lonely.

During the day one has to watch the hybrids but at night that is not necessary. Normally a bear, a tiger or a jackal cannot kill a hybrid; the dogs will hear them and start to bark and then we shout until they go away. However, when I was a child one of our hybrids was killed by a tiger but only because he had wandered off alone at night, far from the *goth*. In the high pastures we don't usually tie them up at night, only near the village where they can damage the crops in the field. I am not afraid of tigers because they don't normally attack people — but I'm terrified of ghosts even though I have never seen one. I stay inside the *goth* when I am afraid.

There is always the worry that a hybrid might be lost and usually at least one a year dies after an attack by wolves, a fall from steep crags, or because of illness. If an animal becomes sick we call the shaman and if it is an evil spirit that is causing the problem he throws clay at the beast. Sometimes the animal recovers and sometimes it dies. If one loses too many hybrids one can become bankrupt.

Festivals

Once a year all people up in the high pastures celebrate the festival of *Erzang* in the month of June with three days of dancing and local beer. All people from nearby *goths* gather at a place high in the mountains and the lama comes to perform a ceremony. Besides this we celebrate the Hindu festivals of *Tihar*, *Dashain* and *Sangrati*: although we call ourselves Buddhists there are many different kinds of people living here in the middle of the mountains and we celebrate each others' festivals which is why we whitewash our house at *Dashain* and perform the *Tihar* ceremonies of *Laxmi Puja* and *Bhai Tika* as well. I believe in reincarnation but despite what the lamas teach, I don't think it will happen in my case as I have not practised hard enough.

Up in the mountains we would sometimes gather together with our friends from neighbouring *goths* to chat and drink local beer but this was not possible too often because the working day started so early. I used to get up at sunrise and the first thing I did was the milking. I then had to give the animals salt and let them graze, and after that I would make some tea and the morning meal of *tsampa* or *dhindo*, a kind of porridge made from barley or maize flour. Then I had to fetch firewood and fodder. If I had to go a long way to do this, then I would have to cook the dinner very quickly once I got back, since the water and cooked grains for the hybrids has to be ready before they returned to the *goth*.

Once it gets dark, the crossbreeds come back by themselves and we'd give them their food together with some cut grass. I always ate my evening meal while they were eating theirs, then I would milk them and boil the milk before going to bed. Once we started selling our milk to the factory we stopped making cheese and butter in the morning. This made life a little easier as we no longer had to carry around the many big pots necessary for boiling the milk and making the cheese. It also meant that we could meet our friends in the factory and enjoy a chat. The milk had to be carried a long way, but selling milk rather than cheese was slightly more profitable. However, even then we could save only very little money. If I had any spare time I would make *lukuni*, a kind of woollen jacket, and baskets made of bamboo.

Lamseki in her kitchen

Nowadays a lot has changed. There used to be always plenty of grass, but now because there are so many *goths*, there is not enough. The yak crossbreeds even uproot the growing grass. It is no longer possible to save grass for the next year, and with so many people chopping the trees, the wooded area with fodder trees suitable for the animals has became very small.

A New Way of Life

Last year we decided to end our way of life up in the high pastures mainly because of our children's education. Besides, my mother is now too old to look after our sons when we are in the *goth* and it is impossible for them to attend school from there, so we sold all our animals. At that time I was pregnant again and gave birth twenty days after we had settled down in the village. I have started taking some birth control pills to avoid becoming pregnant again. Now that we have two daughters, our family is complete. I started farming from last monsoon and am finding it difficult because I am not used to this kind of work. I much preferred the life in the *goth* — the amount of work is almost the same but I liked being up in the high pastures and I miss all the milk products that we could eat up there.

This year I voted for the first time in my life. I had heard about an extreme political group called 'Mashal' who boycotted the last election, so when people came to collect my vote I played

The milk is boiled every day

a joke on them and said that I was also 'Mashal' and, therefore, could not vote! People representing the parties with the signs of a sun, a plough and a tree all came to ask for my vote. They all say that their party would make life better for us, but how do we know who is speaking the truth? I know nothing about politics or parties but my son asked me to vote for the one with the sun emblem because it is his favourite party, so I did so.

About five months ago my father passed away. He had become thinner and thinner, until in the end, he could not eat any more. I tried to insist that he eat at least a little food but he took only alcoholic drinks. Eventually, he died and was cremated — I was so sad. Sometimes I am afraid that something awful will happen to my small children as well. I also worry when my boys fight in school.

Our future is uncertain, as neither in the high pastures nor in the village could we save any money. So, now I would like to borrow some money and start a shop or a small tea stall in Charikot or Kathmandu. However, my children and husband don't want to leave the village. My husband says that maybe it is best if he goes away from the village for some time to earn some money then we can save something and can all go with him. Both of us are illiterate so we don't know much. We are certain of one thing however, and that is we have to send our children to school so that they can have jobs. I hope in particular that my son, Pasang, will be able to get a job in a government office.

Six months later Lamseki had moved with her family to Kathmandu to start a teashop, although her husband was not enthusiastic about the idea.

Two of Lamseki's Songs

The first time I was born as a girl,
The second time I was a girl again,
I do not want to be a girl again,
The third time I want to be a boy.

That rain must fall I can accept,
But do not let the hailstorm come,
My parents may call me names
But let not the rest of the world do that.

— *Eva Kipp*

98

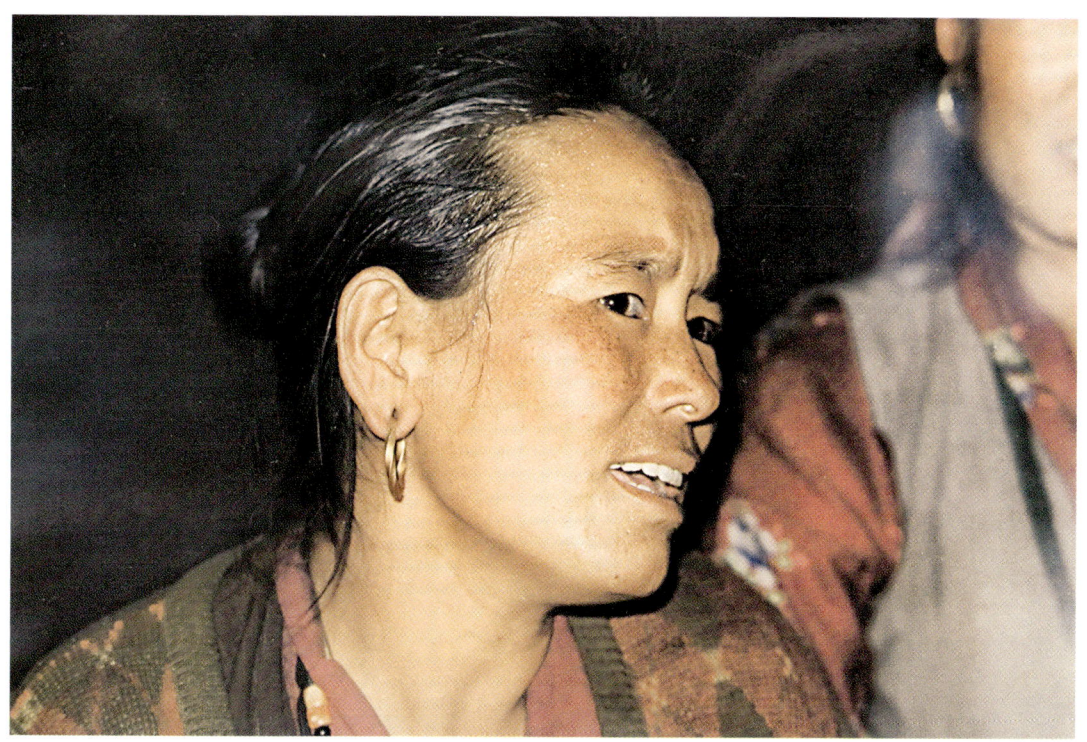

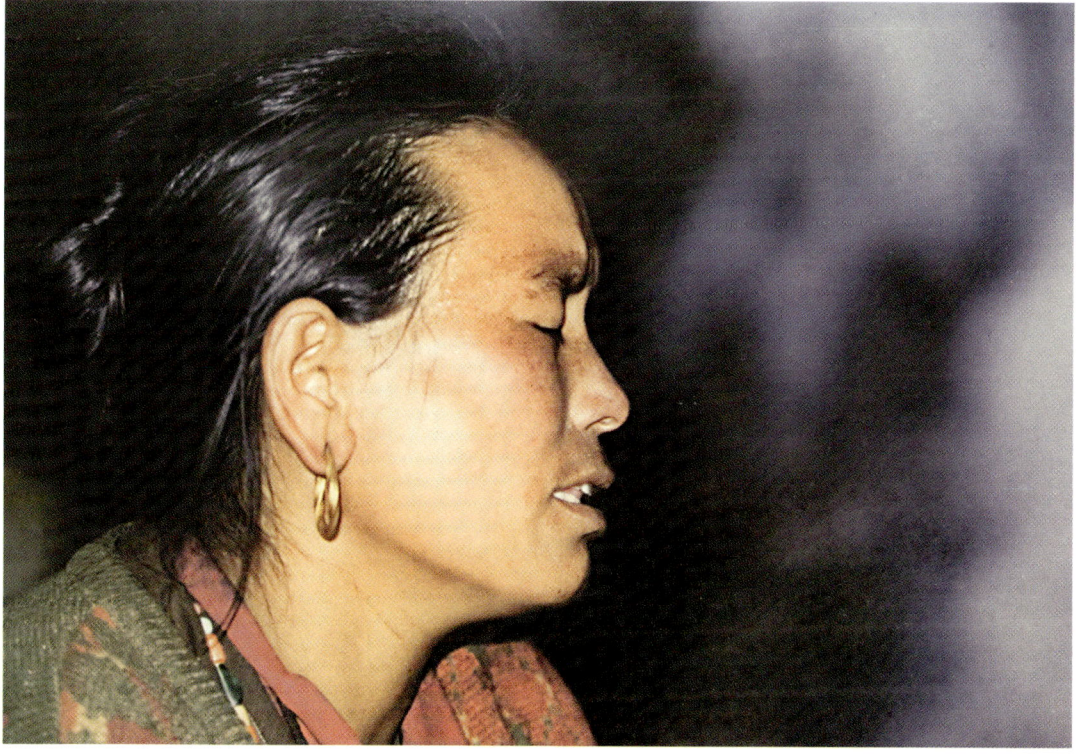

Lamseki singing: 'I do not want to be a girl again'

Rags to Riches

9

Dolma Lama

Rags to Riches

FOR THE LAST couple of decades urbanisation has been increasing in Nepal. About two-thirds of the population in the remote areas lives below the poverty line and harvests no longer provide enough food to meet the needs of a family. Cash is also required to purchase commodities such as sugar, which were previously acquired through the barter system and which are now considered necessities of modern life. So, many village men and women are now forced to migrate to the urban areas of Nepal or India to seek alternative means of survival. Of these migrants, one-third moves down to the Kathmandu Valley and one-half to the rapidly expanding urban areas of the lowland Terai.

Although it is still not regarded as fully acceptable for women in the family to work outside the house, as it has a negative effect on the family's social status, the woman's extra income is often necessary in order for the family to survive. In many cases there is no other breadwinner. If widowed or deserted by their husbands, these women have no choice but to work to support themselves and their children. Most women who enter the workforce do so out of sheer necessity and are prepared to accept lower than average rates of pay. Their need to work leaves them open to exploitation and discrimination by factory owners, especially in the carpet industry where women and young children are engaged in highly skilled weaving for long hours in poor, cramped working conditions, yet are treated and paid like unskilled labour. More than half of the carpet workers are young women and one-fifth are children.

Dolma Lama

Dolma Lama has not always lived in comfortable surroundings. She was born in 1963 in the small Sherpa village of Yalsa, in the Helambu hills northeast of Kathmandu, the fifth of eight children from a family of poor subsistence farmers. When she was nine years old, Dolma was sent to Kathmandu to earn money for the family. Like thousands of other Nepali girls and women she left the safe environment of her mountain village to work in the carpet industry in Kathmandu where she was employed on a piecework basis alongside men who were permanent employees.

When we first meet Dolma, at home in Boudhanath, Kathmandu, she is dressed in a traditional Sherpa costume and is wearing colourful make-up. She is preparing a fresh brew of butter tea by churning green tea, salt and butter in a long wooden cylinder. The house is filled with the sound of sawing and carving emanating from the workshop, which Dolma's husband has established in the courtyard. Inside the house a huge Buddhist shrine forms a splendid centrepiece in the main room together with a television set and a video recorder. The walls are adorned with photographs of Dolma in traditional dance costume, reminders of numerous performances both on television and on the stage. We sit and listen as she recounts her life story in a long, uninterrupted stream of words.

Dolma Lama Tells Her Life Story

Working Girl

The village in which I grew up had just nine houses and was situated in the middle of the woods. My parents had eight children and it was my duty along with my younger sister's to tend to our thirty-five sheep. Early in the morning we would have a snack and then take the sheep to the forest. We would come back around noon for our meal of *dal bhaat* and vegetables, and again return to tend the sheep in the afternoon. I was always afraid of treading on snakes that we knew lay hidden in the grass and during the monsoon there were greater difficulties because of the heavy rain and the leeches that clung to our bare legs. Using a jute bag to protect ourselves against the rain, we would sometimes get so tired we would forget that we were wearing it and would fall asleep with the bag still on. If there was no work at night we had time to play. We built houses and shelters out of stones and pretended there were pots and pans or cattle inside.

I greatly admired those local boys who went to school and wished I could be like them. Without telling my parents I went to school for two weeks; I secretly stood outside and watched what was going on but then my parents discovered what I had been doing and told me that

Dolma Lama

there was no point in going to school because I would go to another family after marriage. Besides, it was a girl's duty to take the cattle out for grazing, fetch water and wash dishes. What's more, the village people said school would ruin a girl's character. After that I only visited school whenever there was a dance performance; I loved to dance and did so whenever I got a chance. I danced at the *Losar* festival, which celebrates the Tibetan New Year and at the Sherpa festival of *Nara*, also at weddings, and at the *Ghewa* ritual which honours the dead.

Money Problems

Our family had a little land on which we cultivated potatoes, radishes and maize. If there was a good harvest we could sell some potatoes, but some years we didn't even have enough to eat. We needed money to buy cooking oil, sugar, soap and clothes. Money was also needed for the expensive annual feast of *Chhiju*, which was organised in turn by each family in the village. One of my older sisters had been supporting the family for some time by working in the carpet industry but that stopped when she became mentally ill.

When I was nine years old my father announced that now, I too, had to work in Kathmandu. I felt happy about my father's decision, as I envisaged Kathmandu as a kind of paradise. When I saw people wearing smart clothes I always dreamt that, one day I would go to Kathmandu and earn enough money to dress like them. I was given a pair of shoes for the first time in my life and set off in high spirits to Kathmandu together with my uncle who had a small carpet factory.

We walked for three days, at one point crossing a swollen river where the bundle of maize I was carrying fell into the water. While walking towards Kathmandu I started to worry about how I could manage without the maize and what I would find to eat in Kathmandu. Eventually I arrived and I remember pressing myself against the wall of a house staring at the vehicles. They seemed as big as houses, moving by themselves and I wondered why the people inside did not fall out. At night everything was lit up. At first it was all so exciting but very soon I started to feel homesick and missed my mother.

Factory Girl

In the carpet factory I lived together with seventeen workmates. Three of my colleagues were from Helambu; the others were Tamang girls. The factory was on the ground floor and we cooked and slept on the first floor. I had a comfortable straw mat, a jute cover, a bed sheet, a blanket and a tin box provided by the owner, in which I kept my things. We each had our own kerosene stove which we put aside at night to make space for our beds. I did my own cooking, usually a simple meal of *dal bhaat*. On some rare occasions some of us managed to get vegetables which we shared together. Often we would work until ten in the evening and would only have tea and bread before going to sleep. At that time bread only cost just over one rupee a loaf.

Normally the factory owner would only pay just before I went back to Helambu. However, if I needed to buy something, he would give me what I needed. One of my younger brothers came to Kathmandu and I was able to pay the twenty-five rupees fee to send him to school. Father visited us from time to time. He brought us potatoes and I would give him some money and special food for *Losar*. At that time I was earning three hundred rupees per month but it was not enough. My hands were often covered with sores from the rough wool we used to weave the carpets with. My fingers became deformed and my eyes started to ache. I worked in three different carpet factories for a period of seven years and then I left for Helambu.

A Thousand Rupee Note

Soon after I arrived back home my brother-in-law returned from India. He said that many people returned from working in India with four thousand rupees. I was amazed! I had never even seen a thousand rupee note. Father made up his mind that we should all go, and two of my brothers who did not want to go stayed to look after the farm. I hesitated at first but my father insisted that we leave, as the temptation of so much money was too hard to resist.

Upon arrival in India the first job we found was in the fields sorting potatoes. We also did weeding work in an apple orchard, transplanted seedlings, and my mother earned some extra money by selling home-made *chhyang*. Then, about four months later, we heard that a lot of money could be earned by black-topping and maintaining roads in the mountains so the whole family walked for three days through the snow to Kashmir. It was not, however, a big city area as we had imagined, but a remote mountain area where a new road and an irrigation canal were being constructed.

It was in Kashmir that I met my future husband. We both worked on the road, and on our one free day a week we cut grass to earn extra money. When he became a contractor he employed our family. After some time he asked me to marry him and, when he noticed my reluctance, he threatened to fire my relatives if I refused. He asked my parents permission and they agreed. They thought I wanted to marry him but I really didn't like the idea of getting married, especially to a man nine years older. I couldn't stop worrying about how I would manage the household jobs, since I was not used to doing that kind of work. I was not happy at all, but nevertheless, we got married.

Back Home

About six months after our marriage my husband became very ill and couldn't even walk. Eventually, due to my care and treatment by a *jhankri*, he recovered but he was shaken by the experience and decided we should return home. We left for Helambu with a total of twenty-five hundred rupees.

We had only been back in Helambu in my husband's house for about a week when my husband left to do carpentry work in other villages. I was left all alone in the house, as my in-laws lived quite far away. I had come to a family poorer than my own and had to do all the farming jobs by myself. I wasn't used to that; I didn't even know how to milk a cow or how to harvest the crops but I solved the problem by asking the other village women for support and we helped each other with the harvesting.

A year and a half later I started to have terrible stomach pains. At first I thought I was very ill, but later that night I remembered my mother telling me how much it hurts to have a baby and I realised that is what it must be. One night, I gave birth to a son on my own, but because I had no idea what to do, I just left the baby with the umbilical cord attached. At daybreak, when I heard somebody whistling outside, I called for help. Seeing me in that condition the villager told me the baby would die if nothing was done so he called someone to cut the cord with a *khukri*.

Return to Kathmandu

After two-and-a-half years in the village I began to feel I could have a better life in Kathmandu since I was skilled in carpet weaving so I discussed it with my in-laws. They were not very keen on the idea but I decided it would be best if I went. I left our cattle with my sister, took my one-year-old son, and left the village.

I travelled to Kathmandu together with a girl from the village and she took me to where she was staying. It turned out that she was a prostitute and that we were in the house of a pimp. The girl was treated quite well but I was not, presumably, as I looked rather dirty. So early next morning I set off to seek work in my uncle's carpet factory. He told me flatly that he could not employ married women, gave me twenty rupees and told me to go back to Helambu.

I tried to find my husband at Boudhanath, a place many Sherpa people frequent. Just as I was getting desperate I saw him rounding the *stupa*, and he took me back to his completely empty room. A kind Buddhist lama gave me some bedding and a few pots and pans. Again I was alone, as my husband worked elsewhere, and since he didn't give me any money I was forced to look for work. I eventually found a job in a Tibetan carpet factory, where they allowed me to work with my son tied to the loom by a long rope. I worked all day and often at night as well, sometimes only sleeping for three hours a day.

A year later my husband started a small carpentry workshop. He took a loan from the monastery and built the house where we now live. However, at that time he lived together with another girl and he started to treat me badly. He did not even visit me in the hospital when I gave birth to our daughter a year later. I was very sick and weak and a friend from back home in Helambu had to help me to go to the hospital. That was the unhappiest time of my life. It was only when I became pregnant for the third time, some four years later, that my husband and I

Dolma near Boudhanath

started to live together happily. My sisters chased the other woman out of the house and then my husband started to take care of the children.

A Better Life

I decided to stop carpet weaving; I didn't see why I should continue to work so hard and started to think about other, easier ways of earning money. I travelled up to Tibet and brought back goods to sell in Kathmandu, on one occasion earning sixty thousand rupees by trading in semi-precious stones. I also help my husband to deliver his carpentry goods to our clients. We have taken several loans to improve our workshop, and at last we don't have a problem making both ends meet. We can now afford to send all four children to the expensive Tibetan Buddhist Dorje School. We also support my parents and my husband's sister with her ten children.

Looking at my children I see that life has changed a lot in a relatively short time. As a child I never had shoes and good clothes and was not allowed to go to school. I used to fight with my brothers and sisters for yesterday's leftovers. One of my brothers was sent to a monastery when he was only eight years old simply because there was not enough food. Nowadays, my children expect me to give them money to buy snacks at school and they see all kinds of films on television. Despite all these changes I firmly believe that my children should be taught about religion.

Dolma and her family eating *dal bhaat*

Dolma dancing

In our village people still give a lot of respect to villagers who have studied to become a lama. Personally, I still worship every day and regularly go on pilgrimage.

Movie Star

The happiest moment of my life was when I appeared on television for the first time. We heard that people were being invited to perform traditional dances on television, so as I have loved dancing all my life I decided to take part. When people saw me dance I was asked to appear in other programmes too, and on one occasion I was asked to tell the story of my life. These days I do stage performances, which pay the best. Sometimes I dream of being a movie star or publishing a book about my life. I would love to see my son become a movie star or a dance master; maybe he can go abroad and earn a lot of money as a dancer. One daughter could be a seamstress and the other a policewoman. I would like to send at least one of my daughters abroad to study but my husband says it is far more sensible to use the money to build her a house.

Dolma's Song: 'The Shaman's Advice'

When sitting and thinking all the time,
you will be bored.
When you walk your feet might hurt,
but do not keep on worrying
because you will die sooner.

— *Eva Kipp*

A Sheltered Existence

The Bigou monastery with the nuns' houses in front

10

Sherpa Omu and Tupendiki
A Sheltered Existence

 UNTIL THE FIRST nunnery was constructed near Tengboche, Solu Khumbu in 1925, it was not possible for a nun to lead a full monastic existence in Nepal. Nowadays, although estimates vary, the total number of nuns in the country is probably only about twelve hundred of whom many are Tibetans who fled their own country after the occupation in 1959. There is also a growing number of western nuns as well as many of Nepalese origin.

The Tashi *gompa* or monastery was founded in 1932 and is situated high in the mountains to the southwest of the Gauri Shankar range at an altitude of 2,600 metres. Below the *gompa* lies the village of Bigou, a settlement of Sherpa and Tamang farmers.

The complete translated name of the Tashi gompa is 'The Pleasure Garden of the Immortal Good Fortunes'. In the early part of the century Nyima Pasang, the headman of Bigou village, requested Lama Sherap Dorje to build a monastery in the area and offered the land where the *gompa* now stands. So with the help of the villagers, and outsiders, buildings were gradually developed into the present-day complex of main temple, library, kitchen, guest rooms, nuns' quarters and an enclosure for the big prayer wheel.

At Tashi each nun has her own cell where she can sleep, cook, study and receive guests; close to her room every nun has her own small kitchen garden. Most receive support in the form of food and money from family members and those who are 'fully integrated' nuns also receive a share from the harvest and the donations to the *gompa*.

The nuns of Tashi *gompa* practise Kargyng Pa Buddhism guided by two *guru* lamas or teachers, Lama Drukpa Rimpoche and Kutshu Tetsu Rimpoche who live in Swayambunath, one of the most important monasteries of the Kathmandu Valley. When a woman wants to enter the *gompa* as a novice she must seek the permission of the Guru Lama. If accepted, her hair is cut as a symbol of renouncing secular life and about a year later, she attains the status of *gyengi* or 'living by virtue'. When the nun has adequate knowledge of the scriptures, she may take the *rabdzung* vow, which confirms that she is totally committed to a religious life. Afterwards, according to seniority, the nuns are required to fulfil various posts for a period of eight to eleven years.

Young girls decide to join the *gompa* and dedicate their lives to *dharma* for different reasons. Some families send their daughters there when they are about eight years old, although most of the girls are between eighteen and twenty-five when they join, often against the wishes of their families. Older women turn to a religious life usually after the death of their husband. The nuns play a subordinate role to monks as defined in the 'Eight Rules for Nuns' by Lord Buddha. Their work in the past focused on contemplation and physical labour rather than scholarly exercises which was the domain of the monks. However, it is possible these days for dedicated and able nuns to do work of great religious significance.

Making sculptures for the evening ceremony

Many decades ago nuns lived a life similar to that of the Hindu yogis, meditating in small caves or walking the pilgrim routes until the first nunneries were built. Over the years the life of the nuns in Tashi has become easier. They no longer have to carry out heavy construction work or labour in the fields, they can now buy things in the *gompa* shop and receive tourists in the guest rooms. Young nuns now have access to modern technology such as tape recorders and television.

Early in the morning the haunting sound of trumpeting conch shells awakens us to a new day in the *gompa*. The monotonous, uninterrupted chanting of prayers emanates from the temple hall, and stoves in the nuns' quarters are lit to prepare the morning meal. The place becomes a hive of activity as the nuns go about their daily chores. The head nun is carefully watching how a novice reads the text of a prayer. Sherpa Omu is busy tending her kitchen garden; another nun is sewing a new piece of maroon cloth. The rhythmic sound of prayers reverberates from a neighbouring house. One nun is fashioning small figurines from flour and butter for a special ceremony; another carries a huge basket of radishes to the tap to clean while others wash their clothes.

Sherpa Omu

Sherpa Omu was born in the village of Bigou fifty-one years ago. While she was still a baby her father left her mother, who later married again, only to be deserted for a second time by her second husband as well. Thus, Sherpa Omu grew up with just her mother and two sisters, and she and one of her sisters decided to join the *gompa*.

Sherpa Omu has already fulfilled all the necessary official positions in the *gompa*. Due to her thorough knowledge of the scriptures used in the monastic services and her popularity, she became deputy *umse* or head nun when she was only thirty-five years old. She is the only nun at Tashi who is sometimes asked by the Guru Lama to help officiate at major rituals taking place in other *gompas* or in the houses of important people.

We talk with her in her tiny room. Inside there are decorated cupboards and shelves displaying many prayer books and a few books in Nepali. Sherpa Omu, however, is quite reticent and does not wish to reveal the full extent of her knowledge. She politely evades the questions she prefers not to answer, especially the personal ones, but expresses her opinions with great clarity when we discuss matters concerning religion and belief.

Sherpa Omu

On one occasion when we were leaving the *gompa* after the afternoon *puja* there was a most spectacular sunset above the mountains — the clouds appeared in a splendid array of red and orange. Sherpa Omu was standing on the steps of the *gompa*, transfixed, and asked, 'Can you also see such a wonderful thing in your country? Do you have this too?'

Sherpa Omu Tells Her Story

My Wish to be a Nun

Since my childhood I have wanted to become a nun because I felt somehow that it was the ultimate religious fulfilment. It is said that whatever things you taste while you are still very young and don't fully understand, you will like in the future. That is probably why I still wanted to be a nun when I was eighteen years old. At that time I thought: 'If I can lead a good, peaceful existence now and dedicate my life to religion, then, when I am born again, my next life will also be good.'

I didn't know anyone when I first joined the *gompa*, but when a new nun arrives everybody comes to have a look and, later on, I became friends with some of them. My best friend now lives next door. We take turns in cooking and she takes care of me if I am ill. I didn't really miss my family because I was allowed to visit them whenever I wanted and, besides, the *gompa* is just

Nuns praying during the evening ceremony at the Bigou monsatery

119

like a big family. For instance, the younger nuns fetch water and do the cooking for the very old nuns who cannot work any more. A nun is entitled to have friendships with people outside the *gompa*. I even have a special friendship with a German lady, sanctioned by a ceremony twenty-five years ago. Sometimes my relatives come to see me here and I can go to visit them when they are ill.

Daily Duties

When I first came here there was always work to do from early morning until late evening. We worked in the fields belonging to the *gompa*, but nowadays this is done by hired labourers. We even carried the stones, mud, water and wood that were needed to construct new buildings. The highest and lowest quarters where the nuns now live did not exist then. My days were rather full; I had a teacher who taught me to read and I then had to learn a text by heart until I knew it, then I would get another. I had to make different kinds of *tormas*, which are pyramids of flour used in our ceremonies, and I also had to look after the goats, which belonged to the *gompa*.

Nowadays, I teach the Tibetan language and also Nepali in the *gompa*. I have already fulfilled all the official posts here so I can concentrate on other religious activities. The first time I went on retreat I found it a bit hard physically, and it was also difficult to remember everything that my teachers and the Lama had taught me. I now regularly go on pilgrimages; Gaya and Sarnath in India, Lhasa in Tibet and Tilaura in Nepal are some of the places that I have visited.

We don't get many visitors from outside. Sometimes the villagers come here for a *puja* or ceremony of worship and we also go to the village to perform them there. For doing this we get something in return. It is up to the villagers to ask for the kind of *puja* they want. For different occasions there are different *pujas*. Sometimes we perform one for a long life, there is one that we do in the case of illness and there is another one for someone who has died.

Love and Desire

If I remember the troubles in my own maternal home I do not like the thought of being involved in love; it takes you away from practice of your *dharma*. I have committed myself to celibacy. My heart has been given to my *dharma* so I cannot fall in love any more. We nuns do not have the same problems as other women. A husband can beat you, your father and mother-in-law can call you names, you have to look after your children, make sure that they get enough food, and you must work hard in the fields. We nuns do not have to worry about these things.

There are many things that one can like and desire but that is not good for the next life. This also counts for material goods; some people like to have a lot of things whereas others are quickly satisfied. That is everybody's own business. In my opinion, the best motto is 'neither stay hungry nor hoard', just make sure you have just the right amount.

Feelings

I am not in the habit of thinking 'this is good and that is bad'. For me every day is a good day. I don't think bad things about other people. I felt upset when my mother died; I doubted whether she got enough to eat and I was worried when she was ill. Since she and my sister have now passed away I only have myself to take care of; all my worries are gone.

Of course I sometimes get angry! Why shouldn't I? Even *Bhagawan* must get angry when there is too much sin in a village. He then sends disaster and misfortune to the village. I concentrate on the anger and try to persuade myself that it can do no good and it then goes away. It is essential to deal with anger in this way, otherwise one can lose everything because of it. Anger cannot feed you, anger cannot clothe you; it can make you lose all your friends and beliefs and may even cause you to go to hell.

Preparing butter tea

I think that all people can practice their religion either inside the *gompa* or at home. Of greatest importance is the way you feel inside you. You can be a nun without having total belief in your heart. There are even nuns and monks who wear the red clothes but who are mixed up in bad business; they tarnish the name of Buddha. One should never forget one's *dharma*. It is always there, in times of difficulties and times of joy. Even after death it will go on.

I advise young nuns to study hard, to forget their parents and home. They should not go to those places where others gather to laugh and to make fun, but if they do go, then they have to be careful. A young nun can easily end up in a relationship with a man and will then have to give up her life as a nun. I am not in the habit of thinking about my future. Maybe I will get sick or even die; and one day I will for certain. For me, just practising the life of a nun is my future.

Tupendiki

The evening prayers are over and Tupendiki is at work in the *gompa* kitchen. She carefully prepares butter tea and Sherpa dishes for the guests, her cheeks blushing in the warm light of the fire. When these chores are finished she returns to her room where food items and clothes are kept neatly in boxes, and prayer books are arranged in an orderly fashion on the shelves. The smell of the butter stored in her room is gradually overcome by the fragrance of incense when Tupendiki performs her evening worship. After having said her prayers she turns on a tape recorder and starts studying English with the help of a cassette.

Tupendiki is now twenty-one and has lived most of her life in Bigou *gompa*. She enjoys her life but admits to feeling a little insecure. She finds it difficult to answer questions about Buddhism because, as she says, 'I still know very little about it.'

Tupendiki Tells Her Story

The Youngest Nun

When I was a child I used to play inside Tashi *gompa*, which was near our house. My father was a sculptor and carved Tibetan Buddhist texts in wood and stone. I am the eldest in the family and have two brothers and two sisters. One day my friend joined the monastery, and when I

Tupendiki

asked my parents if I could go too, they agreed. I was seven years old when I went to live in the *gompa* and for some time I was the youngest nun there.

When I started, there weren't so many nuns, there were only a few buildings, and in the mornings we didn't perform *puja* together in the main temple. When I came here, I really wanted to learn to read and write, and now that I know Tibetan I am able to read the prayers and feel very happy. Until three years ago I lived with my teacher Sherap Sangu. She taught me to keep *dharma* in my heart, my soul and my brain.

Life as a Novice

After my head was shaved my name was changed several times. Then the time came when I started wearing nun's clothes which made me feel good, to know that I now really belonged to the *gompa*. At the age of seventeen I did a four-month retreat for the first time and found it rather hard. The worst part was bowing down on my knees four thousand times a day — one's feet and hands get so swollen! Sometimes I would visit the four other young nuns who were also doing the retreat. We were not allowed to speak to anyone else apart from our parents. I now look back on the retreat as the most important thing I have done in my life and it must also be good for my next life. The realisation that everybody has to die motivated me to dedicate my life to *dharma* and to meditate each and every day.

Scenes of daily life in the Bigou monastery. Evening in the temple hall *(top and bottom)*

Nowadays, I start studying at four o'clock in the morning and after that I make tea and serve it to the nuns who perform the morning *Tara puja*. When I am free, I too join in the ceremony. The work I am doing at the moment in the kitchen is actually the job of my friend, Tupensjoki — I stood in for her when she was taken ill. My own job has the title 'nirwa'. Together with a senior nun I manage the *gompa*, the kitchen and the shop. It is my first official job, and we have to do it for a period of five years. Most of us are asked to fulfil different jobs during a fixed period of altogether eight to eleven years. For one particular job a strong nun is chosen: she has to replace the water in the fifty-eight bowls near the altar, blow the conch shells in the morning and has to clean the *gompa*. Usually our last job is to be *umse* or head nun for which you have to lead the chanting and recitations and explain the meaning of the texts to the younger nuns.

A Visit from Guru Lama

I was delighted when, last year, Guru Lama came and stayed in the *gompa*. He taught me many things, for instance the story of Gelung Palma, the princess who wanted to become a nun. She suffered a lot and was cured of a terrible disease. She lived a really good religious life. I felt good after hearing this story, and after listening to Guru Lama, I thought a great deal. Before he came it was as if I could not think in the right way. I felt as if I didn't know anything at all.

One of the things the lama told us was that people should not go to the political demonstrations in this area. However, people did not listen to him which made me feel very sad. People from the Congress Party came to the *gompa* and told us to vote for them, then others from the Communist Party came and told us not to vote. They also said that, in the future, we would not be allowed to wear our habits or to perform ceremonies. We would not even be allowed to live this way of life or to build monasteries because it would not be for the good of society. I started to worry. In my opinion *dharma* is for everybody and we practise it for the good of mankind as a whole.

Feelings

I find it upsetting when people say that a nun's life is an easy life. Some people even ask me to prove that certain persons go to hell and some go to heaven! On the other hand, people who talk about Buddha make me happy. I get angry when people say something insulting about me. I sometimes say stupid things too, and feel miserable about it afterwards. In times of trouble I talk to my friends and they usually advise me to keep on practising my *dharma* wherever I go.

My parents live in Kathmandu nowadays. I visit them regularly, and while there, I like to watch television with them. Sometimes I meet boys, too. I flirt with them but nothing more. I am happy in the *gompa* and I hope to live here for the rest of my life. I would also like to die here.

We learn many things here — that we must love animals and those people who suffer during their lives. Here I can do whatever I like; I can meditate, speak to Guru Lama when he is here or go to see my family.

— *Eva Kipp*

A Rigid Hierarchy

11

Maya Devi Bohara
A Rigid Hierarchy

THE CASTE SYSTEM has proved to be one of the main obstacles to the development of the village of Ramrekha in the mid-hills of western Nepal. Ramrekha is a poor village, and to improve its situation cooperation is needed between the high and the low castes. However, the high castes refuse to work together with those whom they consider inferior to them.

Chandra Kala Acharya and Krishna Kala Giri sit on a straw mat in the morning sun discussing the caste problem, which has recently sparked off an angry demonstration by low caste leatherworkers or *Sarkis* who forced their way into the local temple, forbidden to those of low caste, shouting, 'We are equal! We are of the same blood!'

The elderly high caste sisters-in-law condemn this violation and claim that it has caused the goddess of the temple to run away. 'We cannot simply abolish the caste system,' argues Chandra, 'it was institutionalised by our great-grandfathers. If we follow this system we will go straight to heaven when we die,' agrees Krishna. 'We cannot work together with the low castes, as far as development is concerned I prefer to go to my fields and work even harder on my own.'

Women's lives in Nepal are greatly affected by the caste system. Although caste laws were formally abolished in 1963, there has been little change in social attitudes and the system still defines the position of each caste in the social hierarchy as well as specifying the occupations of the caste and their social and cultural norms. Low caste women are still expected to clean their own plates and cups if they eat in a restaurant. To actually be allowed to sit inside is still unusual, as people of low caste are not permitted to touch or go near the food and water of the higher castes.

However a few changes can now be observed, which have resulted in a slight slackening of the more rigid hierarchical system. Low caste children are attending school in greater numbers than before. Since pupils of both high and low castes have to cooperate in the classroom, the younger generation develops a more tolerant attitude. Non-formal education, which enables women from all backgrounds to participate in courses on literacy skills and social and development issues, also has a positive effect on women's attitudes. While sharing their experiences, women from different castes discover they have much in common and may start working together more effectively for the development of their community. Migration also helps to break down traditional attitudes as people move away from the areas where they have been brought up with strict social conditioning and are forced to mix and work alongside those of different caste, creed and even religion.

Maya Devi Bohara

Both Chandra and Krishna are neighbours of Maya Devi Bohara who belongs to the *Damai* or tailor caste. Although the women live in close proximity to one another they have rarely met or spoken. Their dealings have been limited to a few remarks at the public water tap on the subject of purity and the order in which people of different castes use the tap.

To meet thirty-seven year old Maya Devi we leave the bustle of Baglung's main bazaar and walk down a quiet lane, lined by tall bamboo trees, to the village of Ramrekha. Here 'untouchable' *Damais* from the tailor caste and *Sarkis* who work with leather make up the majority of the population, while a few Brahmin and Chhetri families live at the far end of the village. In Nepal, approximately two million people belong to the low or occupational castes, most of whom are impoverished and face discrimination daily in their lives. Only a few children of low caste families are able to go to school. Five years ago Dilmaya Damai from Ramrekha became the first low caste girl to join Baglung Campus for higher studies. This year, out of ninety students who enrolled at the campus, only eight were low caste and all were dependent on scholarships for continuing their education.

According to her father-in-law, who is now ninety years old, Maya Devi is very well off as her family can afford to eat two meals of rice a day. Her husband is one of eight men in the village who used to work in the Indian Army, he is a bus driver now. They can only provide enough food for six months of the year from their land, and his income is badly needed to buy extra food

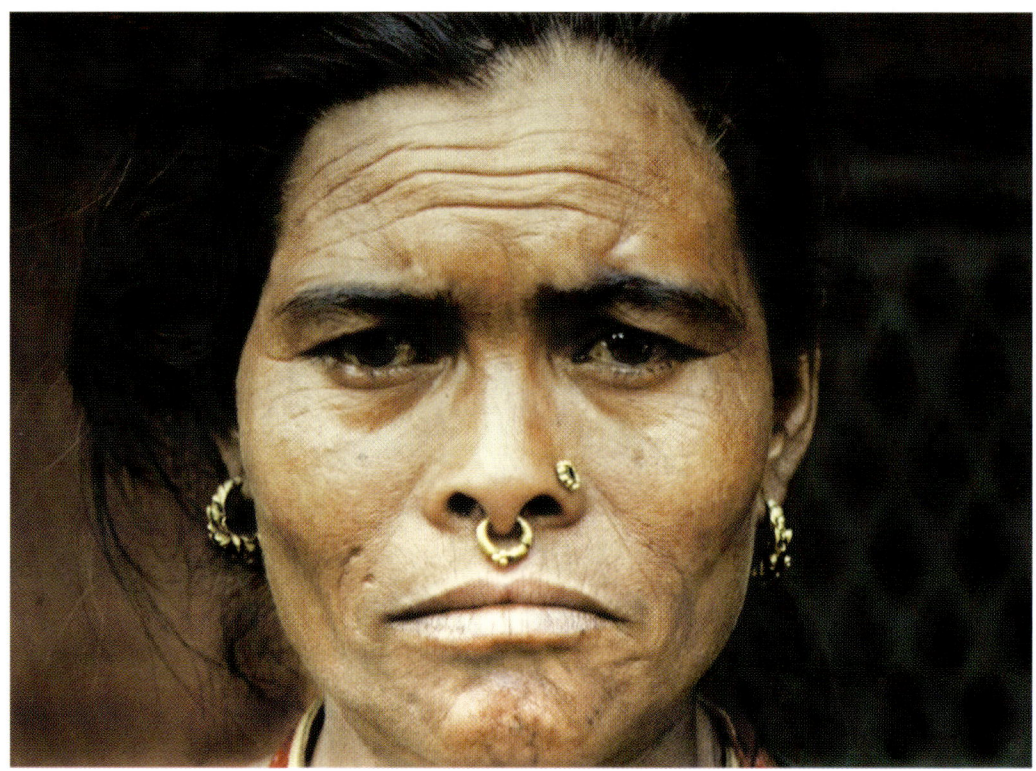

Maya Devi Bohara

and pay for the children's education. Maya Devi sees education as the only solution to poverty and the problems of the caste system. Her dream is to send her children for higher studies at the campus in Baglung or even to Kathmandu so that they may secure a lifestyle more similar to those from the higher castes.

We discuss these issues with Maya Devi in the kitchen of her two-storeyed mud house where she is preparing soya beans as a snack for the children.

Maya Devi Tells Her Life Story

The Truth

I've had no education so I can't tell good stories but I will try to tell you the truth about what our life is like and our many problems. In our Nepal there is so much suffering — I am not exaggerating. A lot of people are landless and have no money at all. Many foreign countries are helping us but the condition of the poorest people does not improve. People are becoming poorer day by day, as they cannot find work and have to take loans. Usually, they cannot repay their debts. So, in some cases, the moneylender goes to the debtor's house and takes away all his property.

In Nepal low caste people face discrimination from the high caste people. People say the whole system of castes was started by a former king but I have no idea whether this is true or not as I cannot read and find out. I thought that our present king was trying to abolish the system.

We women of low castes are looked down upon by those women from the higher castes. At the public water tap the Brahmins tell me not to touch their water pots. They say: 'You can come only after we have finished.' If we touch a very strict Brahmin woman by accident she will immediately perform *chhito*, sprinkling drops of water over herself to reverse the 'pollution' she has suffered. My husband also faces discrimination; when he lived in India he was treated as an equal while in the army, but when he retired and came back to Nepal he found it very difficult to get a job at first. He applied to a development organisation for a driver's job but it was given to a high caste man.

My husband now drives a bus between Baglung and Kakarbhita on the border with India in the east. This work is very dangerous and he cannot spend much time with us, but he has to make money for the family and there is no other work he can do. There are seven of us in the

Ploughing and sowing maize in the family field

family and he is the only one able to earn money. When I met him, some twenty years ago, he was employed by the army and went to Ramrekha on leave. We fell in love and he came to my parent's house to propose marriage. My parents were against it as I was only sixteen at the time, and they thought I was too young to cope with the hard work I would face in the house of my in-laws, so we decided to run away and we got married in a nearby village. I fell in love with him because he had a good job in India and because he was from the same caste and, yes, he was rather handsome too!

A Brief Respite

After our marriage we went to live in India. Life over there was so much better and I just wish we could go back. I travelled a lot through India which I really enjoyed. The army gave us a house with so many taps inside: there was one in the bathroom, one in the toilet, and one in the kitchen. We were given furniture as well. In fact, we were treated in the same way as high caste people. My two eldest children were born in a hospital there because that was the army rule.

After they were born, my husband wanted to be sterilised but I told him not to do it as I wanted one more son. Our culture says that a family should have two sons so that they can perform the many ceremonies necessary after the death of the parents. We tried three times for a son, and the third time we were lucky. You may ask me why this caste system exists; it is a question I ask myself all the time. The gods have not written caste names on our foreheads so why must we take it so seriously? Why is it that a high caste woman can come into my kitchen but I cannot go into hers? God divided mankind into men and women only; we divide ourselves into castes. The colour of my blood is no different from that of a high caste woman; we are human beings and that is the only thing that counts.

In the past the caste rules were far tougher. We had to clean our own glasses when we drank tea in a shop, and even then the shopkeeper would dry the glasses by holding a burning coal near them. Nowadays, the situation is a little more relaxed; at school our children are treated more or less equally and some low caste children even have high caste friends. Nevertheless, we are still not permitted to enter the houses of the higher castes or to touch their food. The business about the food is actually quite funny! We are allowed to touch food which is packaged such as oil and rice, and raw foodstuffs like vegetables and meat, but as soon as this food is unpacked or cooked, we are no longer able to touch it! I really do wonder sometimes: 'What is the difference between a vegetable that is raw and one that is cooked?'

Money, Money

In our village virtually everybody lives under the same conditions — all have to work very hard in order to get food. Uneducated people always work and can think of one thing only — money

Maya carrying a *doko* on the way to the field

and more money. Those who are educated in our caste can get a good job and live the life of a high caste person. They realise the importance of education and send their boys and girls to school, but in our village, nobody of my generation is educated and only seven or eight girls go to school. Except for Dilmaya, no girl from the low castes has gone to study after school. I believe education is very important. I didn't go to school and that's why I cannot speak to you nicely and cannot understand the problems of our country. I can only say 'Namaste' when I meet important people. Whereas, if my children are educated, they can hold conversations with influential people, get a good job and lead a good life; they could also avoid domination by the higher castes. That is why I send my children to school, and to pay for their education, I am prepared to eat less so I can save for their school fees.

I often dream about my children's future. Sachin, my youngest son, wants to be an engineer but I would rather he became a doctor. His school marks are very good and he always talks about studying in Kathmandu. Ranjit, our other son, says he would like to set up his own business, but if he changes his mind, we will do everything possible to help him through university. We can't afford to pay school fees in Kathmandu so we would have to apply for a scholarship. We treat the girls the same as the boys, and if they make it for further study, they could become teachers or nurses.

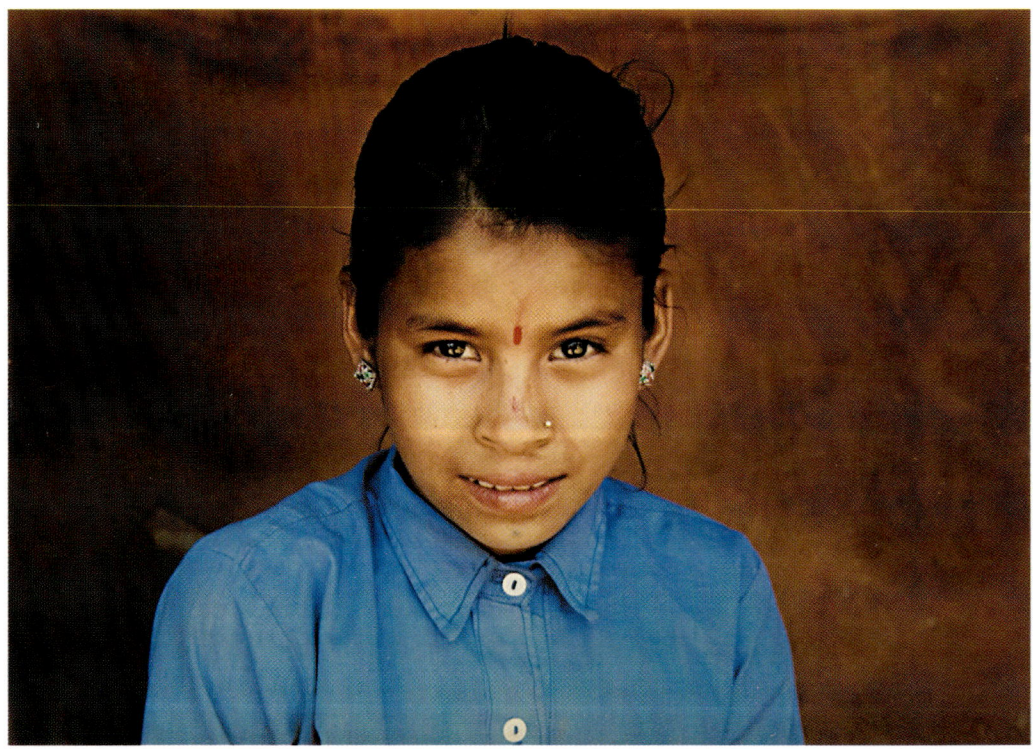

The youngest daughter dressed in her school uniform

Run-away Marriage

Yes, you are right about Sima, our eldest daughter, she did get married nine months ago. It still upsets me. It was just after the death of my father and we were doing the necessary rituals for twelve days. On the tenth day, Sima disappeared. She was still studying in the ninth class at school and I had hoped she would go on to study nursing but she ran away with a boy all the way to Ghandruk, many miles away, and married without our permission. At first I was very unhappy but then I started missing her a lot so I invited her to come over from her in-laws to visit us. I asked her why she had run away and she said she had fallen in love with this boy, who is also *Damai*, and who has passed his School Leaving Certificate examination.

I can't really blame her as, after all, mine was also a run-away marriage. In a way these 'love marriages' are better than the arranged ones since we cannot afford expensive functions and ceremonies. However, if my children are prepared to accept our decision, as to whom they should wed then we will do our best to give them a good ceremony. I am not sure whether my husband will allow Sima to go to campus now that she is married. She belongs to another family now and we have four more children to look after. I doubt if Sima will want to continue her studies as her new family lives in a village where women have to work very hard. The women there cut firewood in the forest and take the cattle out to graze so maybe Sima can complete a tailoring course and set up her own shop in the village.

We Must Work Together

Only when people are educated will our village develop and progress to new standards. It would help if the government could start some industries where we can earn a wage. We would also start a school for women similar to the literacy class that Dilmaya teaches. But first of all, we villagers must start working together. It is a shame that high caste people will not cooperate with us — they refuse to work with us. We low caste people have to work all day and have no time to help each other. It seems that everybody has to solve their own problems.

There is one particular story which my husband tells the children and of which I am very fond.

Once, there was a family of a father, mother and five children but only two of these children were educated. One day the family split up and the children were separated. Eventually the educated girl became a doctor. On one occasion, one of the uneducated boys, who was a servant, became ill and went to the doctor for medicine. The doctor was his sister but they did not recognise each other. When the boy was unable to pay for his treatment, the doctor told him to work as a servant in her home to pay off his bills.

The moral of this tale is that educated people have a chance for a good life while those without end up doing all the dirty work.

— *Lucia de Vries*

Working for a
Better Environment

12

Jagan Gurung
Working for a Better Environment

 THE PICTURESQUE VILLAGE of Ghandruk is situated at a height of 1,936 metres in the Annapurna Himalaya and lies on a sparsely wooded hill surrounded by terraced fields. The 6,000 inhabitants are mainly from the Gurung ethnic group with a few Magars. There are also high caste Brahmins and Chhettris, and low caste people such as *Kami*, *Damai*, and *Sarki* live on one side of the village.

Ghandruk lies on a major trekking route and about thirty thousand tourists visit the village each year. Like many other villages in the area, Ghandruk is now facing ecological problems. The growing local population, which depends on the surrounding forest for ninety-six per cent of their energy needs, has already started to face the consequences of deforestation such as landslides etc. In addition, the needs of so many trekkers have put even greater pressure on the delicate ecological balance between life and land.

Since 1986 the Annapurna Conservation Area Project (ACAP) has been trying to involve local people in activities related to environmental protection of the area through sustainable community development. Local people are involved in all aspects of the process of conservation and development, and ACAP is trying to preserve the local culture as well. In particular, ACAP has stimulated the activities of mothers' groups that have now replaced the *rodi* where Gurungs traditionally entertained themselves by singing and dancing. The mothers' groups were formed when special activities for women were organised by ACAP in 1990 and they now regularly hold sessions of singing and dancing to raise funds for community development projects.

Jagan Gurung

One of the assistants in the Women's Development Section for ACAP in Ghandruk is Jagan Gurung and from her story we can learn about some of the remarkable social and developmental changes that have been taking place in Ghandruk. Jagan receives us inside her lodge dressed in a modern *kurta sulwar* (traditional dress and baggy pantaloon outfit), smart jacket and jogging shoes. Arriving at Jagan's lodge is a delight for the weary trekker, as the lodge is clean and cosy and the flowers give it a cheerful atmosphere.

Jagan takes us on a tour of Ghandruk pointing out that the stone steps we are walking on were provided through funds raised by the women's groups. In the museum she shows us an old lamp that uses butter oil as fuel. 'Look!' she points out 'this sort of lamp was used in my grandmother's time before being replaced by kerosene ones and later by electricity.' We continue on to the part of Ghandruk where the low caste people live and Jagan asks a woman how her baby is doing. She adds, 'The delivery was difficult and we were here until midnight. It was the fourth child and now the family has decided to use family planning.' In the evening we visit a literacy class. In the small room a man is sitting on the bed with a child, while on the floor, six women are slowly reading the text of a book by the light of one electric lamp. Modestly, Jagan tells us about the many activities in which she has been involved.

Jagan Tells Her Story

Tourists

When I was small, groups of tourists used to come to our village sometimes. At that time villagers liked to watch the 'white people' who would build camps near the village and, occasionally, one or two would stay in local houses. I wondered why these people came here: they lived in big cities in big comfortable houses so coming to a place like Ghandruk would surely be very difficult for them. Only when I was older did I begin to understand that, in Nepal, there are places like Ghandruk where there are beautiful natural resources like the Himalayas. Here, there is peace, forest and fresh air and we also have many different cultures. I think the tourists come to see these things.

What the Tourists Brought

I think tourists have brought us a mixture of both good and bad things. They created jobs for porters, guides and lodge-owners and thus helped to increase income in Ghandruk; they also brought many new ideas. However, many years ago we had enough food and did not need to

Jagan Gurung

buy any, but now we have to buy almost everything. When I was small we never used to buy rice and potatoes, but now it is necessary as we have to feed the many tourists that come here too. The price of everything has also multiplied. For example, ten years ago three-and-a-half kilos of rice cost ten rupees but now it costs seventy! The price of potatoes is three times higher and the price of a chicken has gone up from one hundred to four hundred rupees. For poor people this is very difficult.

The forest was already becoming sparse due to the increase in the number of village people using firewood, but it is now almost completely destroyed because so many trees have been cut down to build big new hotels. Lots of firewood is also needed to cook food for the tourists and heat water so they can have a hot shower. By discarding their used cans and plastic bottles tourists have polluted the environment. By the clothes they wear they have affected our culture. Young people like to wear these modern clothes nowadays and the traditional dress is seldom used. Also, tourists who show their affection in public and who are not dressed decently cause great embarrassment amongst the village people.

Youth

My parents' house is just a five minute walk above my lodge. I was born there thirty years ago. I have an elder sister and two brothers who both joined the Indian Army after finishing grades eight and ten at school. My father was in the British Gorkha Army and worked in Hong Kong. Many Gurung people in this region go to other countries to work for the British or Indian Army while most of the women stay in the village, as did my mother, who coped with all the household and farm work on her own. We used to raise cattle and my sister left school after only three years to help my mother at home. After finishing primary school, I went on to secondary school. There were only four girls in my class, as hardly any girl went to school and low caste girls did not go at all. I was the first girl from Ghandruk Secondary School to go to university.

Community Work

I was already doing voluntary community work while I was at school so when I heard about the interesting community development jobs on offer from ACAP I sent in my application. I was accepted and returned to my own village. Usually, local people with a good education do not come back to Ghandruk and most of our teachers come from outside the district.

In the beginning, I found the work very difficult; local leaders and individual husbands did not like the idea of women taking part in the social activities. The women themselves said that they had no time to go to meetings and, when we finally managed to organise one, the low caste and high caste women hardly spoke at all. At the time, I sometimes found it very hard to go to work.

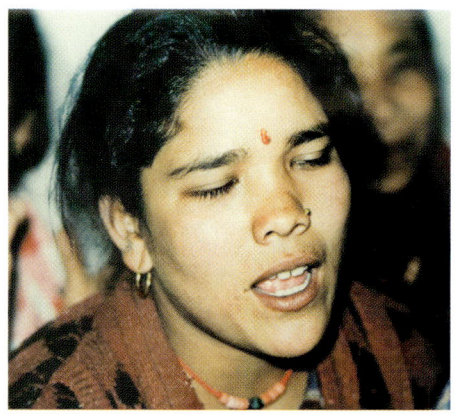

Members of a mother's group in Luang, singing and dancing

Now there are nineteen *Ama Toli* or mothers' groups in Ghandruk alone. Many mothers have now been to adult literacy classes and have graduated from there. Nowadays, many more of them are sending their daughters to school. The mothers' groups collect money by giving song and dance performances particularly if new people, such as tourists, turn up in the village. Traditional songs as well as more modern ones about development are sung so we are also making an attempt to preserve our culture. The groups take decisions as to how the money is to be spent, and on which kind of community activities. Bridge-building, paving the village foot-paths, tree plantations, schools, latrines, health posts, literacy classes and income-generating activities have all been chosen and, just recently, six mother's groups have combined funds to build a day-care centre for the local children.

I am delighted that the local men now admire the women's activities and feel satisfied because the women have done so much towards the development and conservation of the area. The initiative and participation of the villagers has meant that many things have now been realised in Ghandruk. In other areas, too, good women's development activities are going on but I think that what happens in Ghandruk is a bit different. Here the women are involved in overall community activities, not just ones for individual benefit. This counts for all aspects of development here, as we already have committees for lodge owners, electricity, forest management and many more.

Once on International Women's Day the mothers went through the village, and wherever they came across men playing cards and gambling, they took the cards away. They set fire to the huge pile of cards and burnt them all. The men were furious so we organised a meeting in which gambling and alcohol problems were discussed, and from that day onwards, any man who drank alcohol in public or beat his wife had to pay a fine. After one year these rules were slightly relaxed, but up to now, there has been no wife-beating.

The Lodge

I started my lodge with my own savings and some help from my parents in the beginning. I wanted to earn something in addition to my salary, which is not so good, but the main reason for starting was that I wanted to give an example of an ecologically friendly lodge. I now cook on gas instead of firewood, I have made a rubbish pit, and a good toilet; I also cultivate my own vegetables without using chemical fertilisers and I have a solar energy system to heat up water for hot showers.

Before starting the venture I had a good look inside hotels in other places such as Kathmandu, Pokhara, Hong Kong and Singapore to get ideas for my own lodge. I spent six months working in my uncle's hotel after finishing school and learnt the basics of how to run a lodge. I planted flowers near my house, collected books for the tourists to read, bought cloth

Jagan in front of her lodge — Trekkers Inn

napkins, placed heaters under the tables and provided guests with slippers. Now others are copying all the things I do in my lodge. A lone woman works, earns and does some exemplary things and others copy it. I am really happy with this achievement! Last year I also received an award from ACAP for 'Lodge of the Year' for what they called my 'outstanding efforts in promoting sustainable tourism and environmental protection.'

For me these things are the best part of having a lodge but sometimes I wish I weren't quite so busy. My job is already very demanding and every spare moment goes to the lodge. On my Saturdays off I have to work in the kitchen garden and I really wish that people would not come and chat with me so often — I simply do not have time for that. I sometimes wish I had a little bit more time for myself. We have a lodge committee that regulates the room and menu charges of the lodges and I am vice-secretary of that committee. Even now, it is not uncommon for tourists to bargain about such things as the price of a hot shower which is only twenty-five rupees and I do not like that.

Electricity and Back Boilers

There have been many changes over the last few years in Ghandruk. When I was young there were no lodges and no electricity and we did not know how to preserve our culture, forest and

144

Literacy classes in the evening in one of the women's houses

Jagan chatting with women in the low caste section of Ghandruk

environment. The villagers used to wear their traditional clothes but now everyone has western clothes like the tourists and because of radio, television and cassette tapes, traditional dances and songs are gradually vanishing. We didn't know that we shouldn't cut down all the trees but now we are aware about alternative energy, improved stoves, electric cookers and back boilers which all reduce the amount of firewood used.

Now everybody understands the importance of conservation and education. In the old days only boys went to school while girls went to the forest to collect firewood and fodder. Now even the women go to adult literacy classes and learn all kinds of new skills. Everybody has a toilet and people clean the village area every week. Women used to walk a long distance to get water but now they have a water tap either inside their houses or only five minutes walk away.

When I was young, I did not play with or touch low caste girls. I went from school to home and did not meet many other girls from the village, whereas now I know them all. Nowadays low caste girls sit together with others in the school classroom and low caste women sit with the others in the mothers' group meetings. Five years ago this would not have been possible. There are still some differences between low caste women and the others but I hope that these will gradually disappear. For the older generation in the society these old habits are very difficult to change.

Being a Single Woman

I have no wish to get married because life for married women is difficult. If I got married I couldn't continue to work as I do now, as working after office hours and having meetings late at night would probably not be acceptable to a husband. I expect he would look at his watch and ask me why I had come back so late from the office! I would have to devote my time to my in-laws, which means I would no longer be free and be able to give time to the women's activities. I think I would live under great pressure if I had to get married.

On the other hand, if girls do not get married before they are thirty years old, people in this society make a great fuss about it. People will say things behind your back but never in front of you. I sometimes feel hurt when people keep on asking whether or not I have children. At least my parents do not mind that I am still single because they can see the value of the work I am doing and just how much the situation of the women here in Ghandruk has improved. Both my brothers are in India, so from my family there is no great pressure to marry.

I am a single woman who has succeeded in improving her own situation and who helps villagers to improve theirs. By doing this I am an example for other girls too. People say that, even though I am not married, I am doing a noble thing in helping the people of the community. People respect that, and I firmly believe that when more women start to live like I do, people will accept that women can lead a useful life on their own.

A Mothers' Group Song

We have to let our hills stay green,
Let our pheasant dance merry and free,
Showing the colourful beauty of his wings.

— *Eva Kipp*

A Meagre Existence

The village of Kharpel in Humla district
(Photo by Kim Hudson)

13

Bel Maya Shahi and Karmasilla Kami
A Meagre Existence

 THE DISTRICT OF Humla lies in the northwestern part of Nepal on the border with Tibet. Remote and inaccessible, it is at least ten arduous days on foot to the nearest roadhead. The district is populated in the northern parts above 2,500 metres by Buddhist Bhotias, who originally migrated south from Tibet, and in the valleys and lowlands of the central and southern parts, by Hindu Thakuris and Chhetris who fled to the mountains from Rajasthan when the Moghuls invaded India in the sixteenth century. The Bhotias are skilful traders and have amassed considerable wealth in comparison to the Thakuris and Chhetris who trade on a minor scale by taking their sheep and goat caravans south to the plains and north to the Tibetan border carrying salt, grains and wool. Both groups grow a variety of crops including barley, millet, buckwheat and potatoes, but yields are generally poor due to low soil fertility, low rainfall and the sheer steepness of the fields.

Kharpel village is about three-and-a-half hours walking distance from the Humla district headquarters, Simikot, where there is a rough airstrip with flights down to the Terai, weather conditions permitting. The village lies high above the Karnali River at an altitude of about 2,400 metres and is accessible via a rough footpath from Simikot to the north and by a steep climb via Yangtse village from the south. It is built on an incredibly steep, dry slope, which is subject to severe erosion after even the slightest rainfall. The climate varies from cold winters with heavy snowfall, to hot, dry summers with little monsoon rain, as the district lies in the rain shadow of high mountains to the south.

There are altogether about eighty households in Kharpel, of which sixteen belong to low or occupational castes and the remainder to Thakuri families. The village is built in a tight cluster with three rows of houses at three different levels.

Marriage Customs

The Chhetri, Thakuri and low caste people of Humla practise monogamous marriage while the Bhotias practise fraternal polyandry in which all brothers in a family are married to a single wife. Chhetris and low castes generally marry into compatible families in villages a few hours walk apart whereas the Kharpel Thakuris normally arrange marriages with Thakuri families living in the districts of Bajhang and Bajura, which are a twelve-day journey away on foot. This means women rarely have a chance to return to their *maiti* or parental home after marriage but are likely to have a few relatives in the village. The Thakuri system of arranging marriages is gradually changing. Whereas, in the past parents would give their daughters away just on hear-say and would not 'inspect' the prospective home, it is now more likely that the father or both parents will either go themselves to Bajhang to visit the family or send a trustworthy friend. Similarly, families from Bajhang will come to meet the families in Kharpel.

A couple of centuries ago the Thakuris of Kharpel were empowered by the land revenue office to collect grain from thirteen surrounding villages as part of a tithe system. Most of this tithe was handed in to the authorities but a percentage was retained by the Thakuris, and there-fore with this extra grain it was easy for them to compensate for the low crop yields from their steep fields and also pay the low caste families for their labour.

The collection of tithes ended many decades ago and now many households in Kharpel are in deep debt. Even if there is sufficient rainfall only about fifteen families can produce enough food for the year but there is usually too little produced to feed all members of the household and to pay back with interest the grain that has been borrowed from other villages when the harvest has been poor. To offset the shortage, men migrate to India in search of paid labour during the winter months, but some families have to forfeit land or livestock, or may even be forced to go and work as cattle herders or shepherds for those to whom they owe money; sons often inherit old debts that their fathers could not pay. The migration of men for work means that women are left responsible for all household activities and agricultural duties for many months of the year but although they may have access to many of the household resources, very few can exert any control over them except for those few women with their own personal wealth.

The Origins of Kharpel

There is a legend about the origins of Kharpel village. Many centuries ago during the Moghul invasions in India, two Hindu brothers, the descendants of a king, fled eastward to the moun-tains after losing a battle with the Muslims in the Garhwal region of India. They eventually

152

Young unmarried girl in homespun clothes — Kadagaon, Humla

(Photo by Kim Hudson)

came to what is now Humla district in Nepal. One brother settled in Kharpunath down by a small temple by the river while the other settled in Yangtse, roughly half an hour by foot from where Kharpel is situated today. The latter prince then moved further up the steep slope and built the first house of Kharpel village and all the Thakuri families living there today are descended from this one man.

Bel Maya Shahi

Bel Maya lives in a brand new house, which has been built slightly away from the three main lines of flat-roofed dwellings in Kharpel. The house is of a completely different design to others in the village, having a gabled tin roof, wide wooden verandas, spacious rooms and a piped water supply, right next to the house. While servants take care of the housework and the garden,

Bel Maya Shahi
(Photo by Man Maya Gurung)

154

Bel Maya and her husband join us outside. She is attractively dressed in a colourful sari and blouse bought in Kathmandu, heavy gold earrings and many beads and bangles.

Bel Maya Tells Her Life Story

A Good Start in Life

I was born in the village of Chhipra which lies over the other side of the Karnali river from Kharpel. I come from a very wealthy family and when I was married at the age of thirteen, I brought a considerable amount of wealth with me to my new husband's home, in the form of sheep, cattle, horses and grain. My husband already had a first wife but she was very young, had no children and spent a lot of time back home with her parents so he had decided he wanted another wife who would work hard. I got on very well with my co-wife but nine years later she died of bronchitis.

With some of my personal wealth I bought extra land in Kharpel to go with that already owned by my husband and set about increasing the level of crop production. I worked very hard and we had such good harvests, that about twenty years ago, people from up to fifteen surrounding villages would come to borrow grain from us whenever there was a shortage of food. I was very happy to lend them grain at no interest whatsoever, whereas other farmers would demand at least a twenty-five per cent return on what they lent out: to me it just seemed to be a kind of social service. These days my three daughters-in-law do not work as hard as I did; all three of them cannot produce the amount of crops that I used to, single-handedly.

I gave birth to four sons and one daughter but one son died at birth. My husband had studied at the school nearest to Kharpel, which in those days was several hours walk away, and he went on to get a job with a government office. He spent many years working outside the district, and when the opportunity arose to go to Kathmandu, he would take me with him. This gave me a whole new perspective on life and I saw the possibility of a better education for our sons.

The Quest for Education

I was desperately keen for our sons to study, far more so than my husband, who thought it would be too expensive, and I also sent our daughter to school which was very unusual in those days. One son studied up to the fifth class in Humla but he was very bright and the teachers had difficulty controlling him.

I persuaded my husband to take the boy to Kathmandu and enrol him in a good school there, and I sold some of my gold to pay for it. My husband walked with our son, then about nine years old, all the way to Jumla then down to Surkhet and on to Nepalgunj. The boy had to be carried for most of the journey, which took many days through sparsely inhabited country. They took a bus to Kathmandu and the boy was enrolled at a school in the valley.

During the school holidays our son had to be brought home, and from what I heard about the school from him, I made up my mind that it was not good enough for him, so I decided to take him to Kathmandu myself and find a better school. Together with the boy, I made the long trek down to Jumla, crossing high passes covered with deep snow, and down to the flat plains of Nepalgunj to catch the bus to Kathmandu. When we arrived, I took the boy to the prestigious Budhanilkantha School and asked for him to be given a place, only to find that there were no seats available. I pleaded for a long time with the headmaster and described our arduous journey and he finally agreed to admit our son in place of a boy from the extreme west of Nepal who had failed to turn up. Our son was the first boy from Humla to study in Kathmandu and I paid the fees of fifteen hundred rupees per month from my own personal wealth.

Our son did very well at school and eventually went to study abroad. He is now very active in politics in Humla and has started his own non-governmental organisation. Our second son passed his School Leaving Certificate exams in Humla and went on to take the Bachelor of Law Diploma in Kathmandu; he is now a successful lawyer. Our third son is still studying at intermediate level and is setting up his own business while our daughter has married a teacher and now lives in Kathmandu.

In spite of being proud of his sons' achievements my husband also finds it difficult, as they are not around to help him with the agricultural work. The wives of all three sons live with us in this house; one is a teacher at the school and the other two help on the land, but it has been necessary to employ a young boy and a partially dumb girl to do all the extra work around the house. Several years ago we split away from the extended family after bitter arguments between my husband and his brother. Even now the two do not speak, mainly due to political differences of opinion. I used to get on very well with the other women in the house but I do remember my mother-in-law saying that as her younger son had married such a wealthy wife, he could easily go and build a house of his own.

We have had to take on extra people to tend to our livestock; altogether we own about thirty goats, twelve sheep, eight cows, two cross-bred yaks, ten horses, eleven chickens and four dogs. As much of our family wealth comes from my side, I am in complete control of the finances; otherwise I'm sure my husband would have lost most of it in playing cards. My husband does not mind this arrangement, which is very unusual for this area where men normally are in charge of all property and finances. He even tells me that he has been far better off since we got married, so he is happy to let me manage the assets.

I don't, however, strictly control the activities of my daughters-in-law; in the old days young women would not be expected to leave the immediate household area but I don't really mind if any of them go on their own to Simikot or to Kathmandu.

Women enjoying the company of their daughters
(Photo by Kim Hudson)

Karmasilla Kami

Karmasilla Kami lives in the low caste section of Kharpel village. Altogether there are sixteen families of tailors, ironworkers and shoemakers. Their small houses are grouped together at the lower, northern end of the settlement. Because of the steep slope upon which they are built, the continual soil erosion and frequent earth tremors, the houses occasionally start to slide down the hill and have to be rebuilt. The low caste people were not the original settlers but came much later. The Thakuris told us that they were so pleased when the first low caste family arrived that they actually built a house for them, however, the low caste people we spoke to denied this.

We meet Karmasilla on the flat roof of the house where she is sitting with a group of friends, head in hand, pitifully thin and with a look of total despair on her parched and wrinkled face. Her clothes are old and ragged and the pattern on her hand-printed skirt is barely distinguishable. She wears earrings made from old silver rupee coins, a small gold nose ring, a few strands of plastic beads and some silver bangles. She tells us she has hardly eaten anything for the last two days, as there is no food in the house at all.

Karmasilla Kami
(Photo by Man Maya Gurung)

158

Karmasilla Tells Her Life Story

Early Days

I was born in the village of Thehe, which is just two hours walking distance from us here in Kharpel. As a child I remember having plenty of food and enough changes of clothes. My father worked as a blacksmith in the village making iron pots and tools, which he exchanged for grain. For part of the year, both my parents worked in the fields owned by the wealthy Bhotia people of nearby Bargaon village, receiving money and grain in return. When I was fifteen my parents arranged my marriage and I came to live here in Kharpel.

In the early days of our married life we had enough to eat; my husband made tools from iron and also sieves from leather and wood and we farmed our own small plot of land as well as the larger plots belonging to our Thakuri neighbours for which we got an allowance of grain. In the past the Thakuris had a good supply of grain from other villages in the area so they had no problem passing some of it on to us in exchange for labour, however, that situation has changed and these days we all have difficulty finding enough to eat.

Now, when my fields are harvested, I have enough food for just two months — November and December. Along with the other low caste neighbours I have a small area of very steep,

Four low caste women from Kharpel village
(Photo by Kim Hudson)

159

unproductive land on the other side of the village. Recently, when a record of the land owner-ship in Kharpel was made by the land survey office, the small plots owned by those of us from the low castes were measured but not 'passed' by the land survey team so we are not sure whether we actually own our small plots any more. We are poor so we have nothing to give to these officials, and without a bribe they do not complete their work. Other people in the village are able to bribe them and can take the land belonging to those of us who cannot. As low caste people we are dominated and have little control over our own lives.

A Struggle for Survival

Altogether, I gave birth to four sons and three daughters. One son was dumb and died young, but generally my health was good during and after my pregnancies as my husband made sure I had all the necessary food to regain my strength. Providing good food to the new mother is con-sidered of great importance in our low caste society and men often take a loan to ensure that their wives eat well at this time. Some women in our village have lost young children but we are lucky to have a local, self-taught midwife here; since she started to help at deliveries, there have been no deaths either of mothers or of babies in Kharpel.

While the children were still young my husband died. He was less than fifty years of age and one of his brothers told me that the many years of working with iron, using old-fashioned meth-ods, and inhaling the fumes had probably contributed to his early death. After that it became a real struggle to feed my family. At that time I could usually find daily work in the fields belong-ing to the Thakuri families or processing their grains but this was only compensated with a grain allowance for the person who had been working, not for that person's entire family, so we had to share that small amount of grain amongst all seven of us. We would eat our *rotis* with salt and chillies and sometimes with wild vegetables, which we collected in the forest. There are several varieties of wild, green leafy vegetables to be found in the forest and a lot of nettles grow around here. We boil them, grind them and mix them together with flour and fat to make them go further.

None of my children ever went to school. In the early days there was no school in the village, and even though one has now been built, there is little chance for low caste children to go to school as they have to tend to the family livestock and work in the fields. I now live alone with one daughter who is partially dumb. She had been married, but her husband disappeared and left her with a five-year-old son. This daughter keeps the three of us alive by husking other peo-ple's grain, for which she receives a small proportion of what she has husked; I do lighter work such as winnowing and sorting grains for which I receive a few handfuls of grain a day.

Although many of our problems here are associated with the steepness of the land, there is one advantage for us and for the other low caste families; many cattle lose their footing, fall and

Sewing a new outfit — Kadagaon, Humla

(Photo by Kim Hudson)

die on the steep slopes and we low caste families collect the carcass, take off the skin for drying, cut up the meat and bones and cook them to eat. There is a pot of bones boiling here just now and we are drying the skin over there on the roof; it will be dried and processed by hand to make sieves. We know that other Hindus revile us for eating the meat of the sacred animal but, if it were not for those dead cattle, we would probably not have survived.

The Problems Continue

My other two daughters are also married; one lives in Simikot, about a three-hour walk from here, and the other in Takla, just around the hill. One of my sons went to India but has never returned and the other two sons work with iron like their father did, mainly from March until June. These two sons have separated from us and live independently in houses they built themselves, but neither of them has enough to eat at home. Recently, one of my sons took a loan from a man in a neighbouring village and then could not afford to pay it back. The lender complained to the police, who came to investigate the other day, but my son had run away and the police decided that as he had already spent the money and had no property to sell, there was little they could do to about it, so they returned to Simikot.

There are few opportunities to earn money in this area. My daughter fetches medicinal herbs from the forest but she sells these in the village for a low price whereas she could get a higher price by going to the market in Simikot. All the livestock we possess is one chicken. I had an elderly cow but it died yesterday morning. I am very upset about that. It is hardly worth raising chickens as the hawks swoop down and take the chicks. The Thakuri children come and steal the chickens at night and their menfolk come and demand chickens free of charge just to feed their guests. My eldest son has a hive of bees, which he keeps just above my house here. The amount of honey the bees produce varies but we can sell one kilo of honey for a hundred rupees in Simikot if we are lucky.

I still make regular trips to my parents' home in Thehe were my brother now lives. It is possible to get a little assistance from this brother as his family has enough to eat. Last year he gave me a new set of clothes, the first I had for some time. I have another brother but I haven't seen him for more than a year. He lives in Shrinagar in the south of Humla as a *ghar juwain*, (a husband who moves into his wife's home), as her family does not have any sons. More than anything, I am worried about what will become of my daughter and the small boy when I eventually die. For me, death itself is not such a bad prospect — it will release me from what has become a wretched existence.

— *Kim Hudson*

At the Gates of Heaven

14

Man Maya Balampaki Magar
At the Gates of Heaven

 THE SMALL VILLAGE of Godak is situated on the hills on the opposite side of the river to Ilam in eastern Nepal. The villagers are mostly Magars and Brahmins who cultivate maize, rice and millet. The eastern part of Nepal has a long history of development interventions, partly due to the relatively early construction of roads into the hills which improved access to the area.

For the last eight years the Mechi Hills Development Programme has been using an integrated approach to hill area development and, after the construction of many irrigation canals, people have started to cultivate vegetables and a wider variety of other crops as well.

During this period, the Women's Development Project run by the Lutheran World Service was also started in the hilly district of Ilam, where besides non-formal education classes, sericulture has been promoted as an income-generating activity for the village women. Women who are interested receive a month-long training in the cultivation of mulberry trees and rearing of silkworms. They can purchase mulberry saplings at a low price and loans are available to build a rearing house and then they can start rearing silkworms. At the start of the project about five hundred women began rearing silkworms in the area, while about a thousand planted mulberry trees. Those who participated are now earning between 6,000 to 8,000 rupees a year.

Man Maya Balampaki Magar

Man Maya, a resident of Godak, did not at first believe that silkworms could survive on mulberry leaves alone, but once she was convinced she became deeply involved in silkworm rearing. Man Maya is respected as the 'grandmother' of Godak, and has become well known since she became involved in sericulture. Like many women in Nepal, Man Maya became a widow at an early age and at first her involvement in sericulture met with a lot of opposition and prejudice, but it made her strong and able to cope with the problems that come with old age. Indeed, there is little that shakes her nowadays. 'I have nothing to complain about', she says, 'It's only that my sight is not as good as it used to be and I don't find it so easy to carry fodder and firewood as I once did.'

Man Maya is now aged about eighty-four and when we meet her she is happy to stop working for some time to reflect on her long life. Talking about her marriage and about the death of her step-daughter is still very painful but she has come to terms with her remarkable, often tragic life, and looks forward to going to heaven to meet her husband, brothers and sisters again.

Man Maya Balampaki Magar

Man Maya Tells Her Life Story

A Splendid Wedding

I was not even ten years old when my marriage was arranged. My husband was twenty-five and was already married to my elder sister. When, after five years, she did not bear any children he decided to marry me too. I was carried to my new home in a sedan chair wearing a red sari and a traditional cross-over blouse made from three layers of cloth; my face was covered by a red shawl. *Damai* musicians from the tailor caste played music day and night and we danced and danced. After the dancing, poems were recited. It was all so beautiful and it makes me sad when I think of that time.

Those days have gone and they will never come again; they will be forgotten. We don't even have any photographs of the wedding because cameras were not around then. Nowadays, weddings are not so splendid — there are no sedan chairs, no poems and nobody dances all night long anymore. For a dowry, my parents gave me some goats, a few cows and some ornaments such as a nose ring, a chain and earrings. They gave a set of clothes and a golden earring to my husband. When the wedding was over I felt so shy and afraid in my new home that I ran away, back to my parents. It was only three years later, when my husband came to take me back, that I stayed for good.

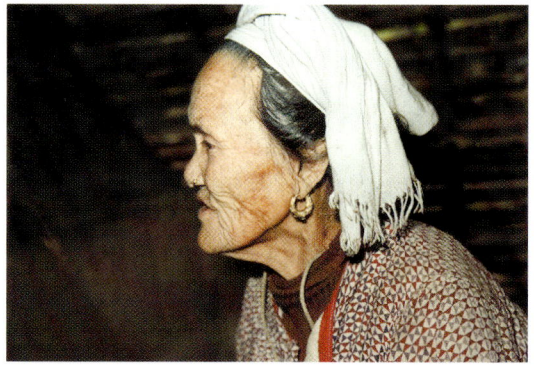

Man Maya telling her life story

Life as a Second Wife

My elder sister was like a mother to me; she did the work inside the house while I was working outside looking after the cattle and working on the land. After three years I gave birth to a son, but he died. Then my sister gave birth to her first child and, in the end, we had many children between us — I think about thirteen — but many of them did not survive. They are gone — gone forever. My sister and I were never jealous of each other. My husband treated us as equals and used to bring presents for both of us. I remember him taking me in his arms and dancing with me. He was so strong and the most handsome of five brothers. I still remember the *puran* ceremony we performed when my husband was still alive, for seven days we stayed beside a river, eating and sleeping there, performing ceremonies and having such a wonderful time together. That really was the happiest time of my life.

Then, when my youngest daughter Urmila was twenty-two days old, my sister died. All of a sudden, I had to do all the work on my own and take care of her children, too. I have always treated the children equally, giving them the same food and the same presents when they got married and they have never complained that I have been unfair. That same year my husband also died and his property was divided into two parts — one for each of his wives.

Widowhood

As a widow one is not allowed to wear beads and gold ornaments or red clothes. People say very

Man Maya in her shop

spiteful things to you when you are a widow. I didn't take notice of what they were saying, for I knew that they would also be in the same position some day — one of the two has to die first. The most awful part of being a widow was the grief I felt at the loss of my husband.

In those days we had a lot of livestock, such as goats, sheep, pigs, cows and chickens, so there was a lot of work to do. My brothers offered to help, but I did not want to bother them as they had their own problems. So, when I could not rely on the man I had hired to cultivate the land, I started to do the ploughing myself. I'm not sure why, but women were not allowed to plough. Villagers started to make comments, until one day the village headman came and told me to stop. I replied, 'Unless you take my children and feed them I won't stop ploughing!' He was speechless and went away.

However, the heavy work became increasingly difficult for me and I started to think about an easier way to earn money. Many travellers pass our house, since it is built at the entrance of the village, so I decided it might be possible to earn some money by selling some goods and that is how the idea of a shop came about. It was the first shop in the village. To start it I took a loan worth ten thousand rupees, which I haven't been able to pay back to this day.

Trials with Sericulture

Do you see the photograph here in which I am pictured together with my cocoons? It is

Man Maya carrying cocoons

168

everywhere in the Mechi area and has made me famous. It all started nine years ago when my daughter and granddaughter got involved in sericulture. I wanted to know if the silkworms could really survive on mulberry leaves and secretly took some home. I kept them in my bed and they turned into cocoons and then into moths; after that I was convinced and started to rear silkworms, too.

During the main rearing season I have to get up at six o'clock in the morning. I feed the silkworms, make the tea and my morning meal, work in the kitchen garden, and in the evening cook dinner. In addition to that, I feed the silkworms five times a day, as I learnt at the sericulture training. My daughter helps me with trimming the trees, which is the only heavy part of the work. Since I am old, sericulture is an ideal occupation for me.

About a year ago I decided to donate the best part of my land to the sericulture project. That was the most suitable part because cars, villagers and visitors who are not used to climbing can reach the place easily. Initially, one of my sons was extremely angry and we had a big argument about it. I tried to convince him that everybody would benefit from the development of sericulture in our village and, besides it would be good for our family name, as in the future everyone would remember us. However, he was still angry, and so I had to give him a piece of land on which he could build a new house. I still remember the day when the land was transferred, I was very ill and they had to carry me down to the roadhead and drive me to the registration office.

How Life has Changed

I was the first to settle down in Godak; five other families followed after me and just look how many houses there are now! We used to graze our cattle in the forest but nowadays they are fed with straw in the stable. We used to cultivate only rice, millet and maize, however, along with development came irrigation and we were able to cultivate other things as well. Sericulture was introduced to the village a few years ago, people also started to knit sweaters and weave carpets. I was born too early for all this change. My grandchildren taught me how to read and write but I've forgotten everything.

Nowadays, rather than working, children go to school, play and do whatever they want. They don't have any responsibilities. Depending on their capacity to learn they have a chance for a better life. I believe religion has changed, too. Everybody is travelling around, and when one is outside, one cannot practise religion as strictly as one can at home.

My Recipe for Good Health

I think the reason why I'm so healthy in my advanced age is that I always cook for myself, even when I travel. I only eat food that we have produced ourselves, and only the rice that is beaten in the traditional way. I never take medicines from pharmacies, either. Even when I was injured in an accident and was given medicines from the hospital I didn't use them — I threw them down the toilet! Honey is a perfect medicine for all sorts of purposes. It is useful for relieving pains and fever and almost all other diseases. I give raw honey containing live larvae to the grandchildren, and it makes them fat and healthy. Whenever I am ill I go to the woods to search for the roots of the *dobi* plant which has red and white flowers and isn't difficult to find. Another good medicine is *hara*, a medicinal fruit, but it has to be heated until it pops and then you can eat it.

Six years ago a minister who comes from our area invited me to go to Kathmandu and I went together with my step-daughter. On the way, near Bharatpur, we had an accident and both of us had to be taken to the hospital in Kathmandu. I had to have stitches in my head but I was allowed to leave the hospital. My step-daughter had to stay. No one ever told me she was in a critical condition but a month later she died while I was out visiting temples. They told me this the following day and we cremated her at the most holy site, the burning *ghats* by Pashupatinath temple. My heart breaks when I think about her; she was so good to me, bringing me delicious food, caring for me when I was ill and always warning me not to work too hard.

A Meeting with Sant Balaguru

Some time ago Sant Balaguru came to Ilam, and my neighbour and I went to the temple to visit the holy man. He told me, 'From your face I see that your heart is very bright.' I told him that it is my last wish to meet my husband in heaven. However, Sant Balaguru told my neighbour that she had a black spot in her heart. It was true because she is bad-tempered, and besides, she relieves herself near the school. I have a good laugh when I think about it, that the school is supposed to be the temple of wisdom and to defecate close to a temple is just not done. That woman is the only person whom I cannot get along with. She is always calling me names and really isn't a nice person at all. She even once said to me that when I die she'd be very happy and would slaughter a chicken to celebrate. I told her that she'd do better slaughtering a buffalo.

I know from the scriptures that we will live eighty-four lakh lives. I do hope I will be reborn as a human being and not as a dog or a cow but that depends on the kindness of God. I hope to go to heaven to meet my husband and sisters. I'm not sure what heaven looks like because I haven't been there, but I once dreamt about it. Eighteen years ago I was very ill and while lying in my bed I had a dream: I met an old man with white hair who wrote my name in a book and then took me to heaven. I was worried, my youngest daughter Urmila was still small, and because of her I didn't want to die yet. We arrived at the gates of heaven which were guarded by two dogs. They started barking and chased me away. Then I woke up and realised with relief that the barking of the dogs meant that it was not yet time for me to go.

I am still alive while most of my friends and family members have already gone to heaven. Five years ago my sister died; my two brothers and other sisters had already died before her. It is hard to be left alone. There are two big wishes that I would like fulfilled before I die — I would like to see a silk factory in Nepal and I would like to pay back the loan which I took to start the shop. There is still time. I think I will live for another five or ten years.

Man Maya's gnarled hands after eighty-four years of hard work

Man Maya's Favourite Song

I went to the garden and plucked the flower,
Thinking of you.
Come to me,
Come smiling,
I am waiting for you,
To give you the flower.
I went to the garden and plucked the flower,
To wear it for you.

I call you,
Come sit with me,
By the tree.
Come to the garden,
And talk with me.

— Eva Kipp and Lucia de Vries

172

Glossary

chaimani	Traditional birth attendant (also see *sudeni*)
chiura	Beaten flat rice
churpi	Hard dry cheese
chhyang	Home-made brew of fermented rice, barley or millet
dal bhaat	Traditional Nepali meal of rice and lentils and sometimes vegetables
Dashain	Most important Nepalese festival dedicated to the Hindu goddess Durga; A long holiday and an occasion for visiting family and exchanging presents
dharma	Religion or truth, applied to both Hinduism and Buddhism
doko	Basket carried on the back and secured with a strap on the head
dhindo	Porridge made from barley or maize-flour
dimzo	Female hybrid from yak and cow
gompa	Buddhist monastery
ghum	Personal rain shield made of bamboo mats and leaves
gupha basne	Rituals indicating a girls entry into puberty, performed by Newars before or during the first menstruation
goth	Temporary mountain shelter made from woven bamboo mats, stones and branches
jhaand	Local beer brewed from maize, rice etc.
jhankri	Traditional village healer who often employs spirits and supernatural powers, variously translated as faith healer, shaman or witch doctor
kanyaadaan	Ritual for giving a daughter's hand in marriage
khukri	Traditional long curved Nepali knife
Lakshmi	The goddess of fortune and wealth; consort of Vishnu
lakh	a hundred thousand (100,000)
pande	Praja term for *jhankri*

173

puja	Worship, ceremonies, ritual offerings and prayers, usually to the gods or to respectful persons
rupee	Nepalese monetary unit, approximately 50 rupees equals one US dollar
roti	Flat round unleavened bread, cooked on open fire and/or griddle
sindur	Red powder placed by a woman in the parting of her hair, signifying marriage
stupa	Large, bell-shaped Buddhist shrine
sudeni	Traditional birth attendant
swayambar	Marriage ritual with exchange of garlands and red powder but without the presence of a priest
tika	Spot of red powder ritually placed on the forehead
tapari	Traditional plate usually made from *saal* leaves
torma	Ritual statue made from flour and decorated with butter designs
tsampa	Flour made from roasted barley, a staple in Tibetan and Sherpa diet

Authors and Contributors

Eva Kipp (*b*. 1947) is not only a talented author and artist (she drew and designed the front cover for the first edition), but also an educational specialist on cultural issues. Born in the Netherlands, she has written a number of books on women, culture and folktales from West Africa, the Netherlands and Nepal. Having previously worked in Europe as a freelance photographer she went to work in Guinea-Bissau (West Africa) for eight

years as an educational specialist and produced several programmes on Africa for Dutch Educational Television, as well as writing books, all illustrated by her own photos or drawings.

With her husband Eric Kamphuis, the Dutch Consul to Nepal and Director of SNV (Netherlands Development Organization), she — along with their adopted four-year-old Nepali daughter Pramila — has lived, worked and travelled throughout Nepal for about four years. She has compiled and illustrated a book of Nepali folktales, *Bahadure Kaila and the White Ghosts* (1993), and is currently working on a second book of folktales with the same compilers,

and is also designing a children's book for young Nepali readers.

Co-author and contributor **Kim Hudson** was born in England in 1957 and is married to a Nepali. She holds degrees in Geology and Rural Social Development, and has been living and working in Nepal for about ten years. She is currently the Community Development Specialist Officer for the Karnali region, Western Nepal for SNV.

Other Contributors

Trained in journalism and peace studies in the Netherlands and the U.K., **Lucia de Vries** (*b*. 1964) is a freelance journalist working in Nepal specialising on development issues, and is co-editor of the Kathmandu based magazine *Face to Face*.

Marieke van Vliet (*b*. 1965) is a Dutch anthropologist who has lived in Nepal for over five years. During this period she has undertaken various research projects concerning women and health and is currently involved with the Biogas Support Programme.

Alieke Barmentloo (*b*. 1964) is a teacher of Language and Health Education, and has worked both in Africa (teaching dietetics), and Nepal, carrying out gender research in the villages.

Other books by Eva Kipp

Bahadure Kaila and the White Ghosts, Nepali Tales (1993)

Forthcoming

The Golden Umbrella, Nepali Folktales
Sunflower: Folktale for Children (in English and Nepali)

Other books of related interest by Pilgrims Publishing

Un Jour a Kashi
Severine Dabadie and Christiane Etchezaharreta

A Day in Kashi
Severine Dabadie and Christiane Etchezaharreta

Returning an Indian Odyssey
Ilaa Dev Pal

Upside Downside
Winona G Campbell

Beyond the Summit
Linda LeBlanc

Sagarmatha: Mother of the Universe
Margaret Jefferies

Kangchenjunga
Tim Hauf